T0393872

Managing Convergence in Innovation

Technology in several forms, especially Information Technology (IT), has a strong tendency to converge at varying degrees. This phenomenon of converging innovation is likely to deepen and widen in the future due to intense competition in global markets. Asian manufacturing firms in particular lead the global industrial innovation. Convergent innovation exists as a constant disequilibrium between reference technology and matching technology; innovations of these technologies occur at different degrees to attain an optimal balance. Innovations as a result of convergence are often beneficial, improving welfare and employment. This book sheds light on the little-discussed idea of convergent innovation with examples hailing from Asia. The book also proposes new theories and investigates convergence at the micro level – guaranteed food for thought for academics interested in innovation economics and management.

Kong-rae Lee is Chair Professor of the Management of Innovation (MOI) Program at DGIST. He received his PhD from SPRU, University of Sussex, UK. He was a research fellow of the Science and Technology Policy Institute (STEPI), Korea, and served as head of the policy division and member of the Korea Academy of Science and Technology (KAST). He also served as policy advisor to Minister of Science and Technology, the Republic of Korea in 1995. His research areas are national, regional and industrial innovation systems, and mega science policies. He has published many books and articles, including the book *The Source of Capital Goods Innovation* in 1998.

Routledge Frontiers of Business Management

Managing Convergence in Innovation

The new paradigm of technological innovation

Edited by Kong-rae Lee

Routledge
Taylor & Francis Group

LONDON AND NEW YORK

First published 2017
by Routledge
2 Park Square, Milton Park, Abingdon, Oxon OX14 4RN

and by Routledge
711 Third Avenue, New York, NY 10017

Routledge is an imprint of the Taylor & Francis Group, an informa business

© 2017 selection and editorial matter, Kong-rae Lee; individual chapters, the contributors

British Library Cataloguing in Publication Data
A catalogue record for this book is available from the British Library

Library of Congress Cataloging-in-Publication Data
Names: Lee, Kong-rae, editor.
Title: Managing convergence in innovation : the new paradigm of technological innovation / edited by Kong-rae Lee.
Description: Abingdon, Oxon ; New York, NY : Routledge, 2017. | Series: Routledge frontiers of business management ; 2 | Includes bibliographical references and index.
Identifiers: LCCN 2016011555 | ISBN 9781138191938 (hardback) | ISBN 9781315514895 (ebook)
Subjects: LCSH: Technological innovations—Economic aspects. | Industries—Technological innovations. | Technological innovations—Management.
Classification: LCC HC79.T4 M34734 2017 | DDC 338/.064—dc23
LC record available at https://lccn.loc.gov/2016011555

ISBN: 978-1-138-19193-8 (hbk)
ISBN: 978-1-315-51489-5 (ebk)

Typeset in Galliard
by Apex CoVantage, LLC

Contents

Figures

Tables

About the authors

George Barnett has been Chair of the Communication Department at the University of California, Davis, 2009–2015. He has served as Chair of the Communication and Technology Division of the International Communication Association, and President of the International Network for Social Network Analysis. He is Advisor to numerous universities, corporations, the National Science Foundation (USA), and Humanities and Social Science Research Council (Canada). His most recent book is *Advances in the Diffusion of Innovation* (Peter Lang Publishing), published in 2011.

Changsu Kim is Professor at the School of Business, Yeungnam University, South Korea. He received his PhD from London School of Economics (LSE), UK. He is a Chief Editor of the International Journal of Information Communication Technology and Digital Convergence. He has been Chairman of the Board of Directors of the Korea Institute of Digital Convergence since 2012, and President of the Korea Academic Society of Digital Business Administration since 2014. He is the author of many articles and co-author of 15 books, including most recently *Big Data Management* at HakHyunSa, South Korea in 2014 and *Digital Business* at Chicago Business Press, USA in 2015.

Guktae Kim is a doctoral research student in strategy and organization at the School of Business Administration, Kyungpook National University. He has published many articles in domestic and international journals including *Asia Pacific Journal of Management, Asian Journal of Technology Innovation*, and *Korean Journal of Management*. He has won four best paper awards from academic societies and international conferences in the past three years.

Fumio Kodama is Professor Emeritus at the University of Tokyo, and also at Shibaura Institute of Technology, Tokyo, Japan. He is currently Visiting Professor at Kwansei Gakuin University, Hyogo, Japan. He was Director of MOT Research Center at Shibaura Institute of Technology in Tokyo. He is the author of many articles and books. One of his works is *Analyzing Japanese High Technology: The Techno-Paradigm Shift* (Pinter Publishers, London, 1991). His works include the book *Emerging Patterns of Innovation: Sources of Japan's Technological Edge* (Harvard Business School Press, 1995).

Kong-rae Lee is Chair Professor of the Management of Innovation (MOI) Program at DGIST. He received his PhD from SPRU, University of Sussex, United Kingdom. He was a research fellow of the Science and Technology Policy Institute (STEPI), Korea, and served as head of the policy division and member of the Korea Academy of Science and Technology (KAST). He also served as policy advisor to Minister of Science and Technology, the Republic of Korea, in 1995. His research areas are national, regional and industrial innovation systems, and mega science policies. He has published many books and articles including the book *The Source of Capital Goods Innovation* at Harwood Academic Publishers in 1998.

Yukihiko Nakata is currently Professor at Ritsumeikan Asia Pacific University. His work experience includes Central Research Laboratories, Sharp Corporation and Sharp Microelectronics Technology, Sharp Laboratories of America as a Director in the USA, and Advanced LCD Technologies Development Center Co. Ltd., Yokohama. He has been engaged in the R&D of electroluminescence (EL) devices, solar cells for eighteen years, and tin film transistors for LCDs for ten years.

Tamotsu Shibata is Professor of Innovation Management, Graduate School of Economics and Management, Tohoku University, Japan. He received his PhD from the University of Tokyo. Prior to his PhD, he did his MBA and worked in the product development department for Fanuc, Ltd., a leading machine tool company. His research has appeared in several leading academic peer reviewed journals such as *Research Policy, R&D Management*, and *International Journal of Technology Management*.

W. Edward Steinmueller received his PhD in Economics from Stanford University. He has been Professorial Fellow at SPRU since 1997. He began his studies in the areas of computer science, mathematics, economics, Chinese language and history at the University of Oregon and Stanford University. He was selected for a chair at MERIT at the University of Maastricht, Netherlands, where he developed a doctoral training school prior to coming to SPRU. He has published widely in the field of industrial economics and social policy issues of the information society.

Chan-Yuan Wong is currently Senior Lecturer at the Department of Science and Technology Studies, University of Malaya. He received his PhD in applied statistics from the same university. He is also an associate for Ministry of Science, Technology and Innovation (MOSTI) and Malaysian Industry-Government Group for High Technology (MIGHT) in several research projects, and IDRC-sponsored projects on innovation policies and inclusive development of Asia. He has published widely in the field of economics of catching-up and development and evolutionary science and technology policies.

Jong-Yong Yun joined Samsung Group in 1966, where he became an executive in 1988 and was promoted to CEO, President of Samsung Electronics in 1992 and Vice Chairman in 2000. During the period he served as a CEO, Samsung Electronics became a world-leading company not only in innovation performance but also in sales and profit performance. He received a prize for The Most Successful Chief Executive Officer in Korea from Korea Management Association in 1998, and was selected as one of the Top 25 Managers of the Year by *Business Week* in 1999 and Asia's Businessman of the Year by *Fortune* in 2000. In 2010, he ranked number two on the Best-Performing CEOs in the World in 2013 by *Harvard Business Review*.

Foreword

One of the most important features of the current wave of industrialisation is the convergence of different categories and processes of innovation. The concept of 'convergence innovation' put forward in this book helps explain how many diverse technological knowledge fields are being combined in order to create not only new products but also new functions, processes and services. But how can we understand, analyse and interpret modern convergence innovation? This is not a trivial question. It goes to the very heart of understanding the so-called Fourth Industrial Revolution described in this book. However, until now, we have not yet had the research needed to understand the processes involved in convergence innovation or the impact on firms, other organisations, industries and nations.

By bringing together a range of new studies of convergence innovation, which build upon the pioneering studies of the past, this book goes beyond the limits of existing evidence, concepts and theories and shows precisely how convergence innovation operates and functions within the modern economy. Focussing especially on the region of East and South East Asia, the chapters contained in the book reveal the nature of convergence innovation and the ways in which it is transforming businesses, product categories and entire industries. The book shows the ways in which firms have learned how to master convergence innovation, and it illustrates, in depth, the networks and communications needed to support convergence.

The book, divided into three main parts, consists of a fascinating collection of papers from different convergence perspectives. Part I concentrates on how individuals and firms learn and diffuse knowledge, generating new convergence innovation processes. We witness how new modes of convergence learning have gone beyond the traditional forms of learning we are familiar with. Learning-by-porting, learning-by-using and learning-by-integration have arisen to develop and diffuse convergence innovations. New products, practices and ideas are created and diffused through networks with particular cognitive processes which enable individuals and groups to create and generate innovations.

Part II provides new empirical evidence to show how very large firms can manage the processes of convergence. Taking Samsung Electronics in South Korea as a case in point, we see how convergence innovation produces difficulties and barriers as well as opportunities. The evidence shows how firms can cope with the anxieties that convergence innovation can produce and how to formulate the objectives and visions necessary for successful change. This part of the book also deals with the navigation of convergence innovation at the meso- and country levels, showing how diversity and non-conformity are essential elements of managing convergence innovation successfully. In the case of Asian countries, a transformational change is needed to overcome the heritage of catch-up competitiveness which, in turn, means that diversification must become an important part of the science and technology policy agenda.

Part III deals with cases of convergence innovation in Asian industries and countries. Intra- and inter-industry convergence are analysed, and five industry types are identified, based on their innovation characteristics. The case of convergence innovation in specialized textile machinery suppliers in South Korea reveals that convergence innovation has continuously increased, in different ways, over the period of 2001–2011. We also see that convergence innovation is linked to city innovation systems in the railway sector, with railway companies pursuing and assimilating new capabilities outside their traditional span of operations.

Interesting policy implications for local and central governments are drawn from the empirical chapters, showing how governments can promote convergence by focusing on seven key dimensions of convergence innovation: spatial, process, user-supplier, R&D, the human side, institutional and cultural. The suggestions represent useful insights for governments interested in pursuing convergence innovation for social welfare and economic growth.

This book is both original and path breaking in its achievements, not only from an evidence perspective but also from a conceptual and theoretical point of view. The work is rich in empirical data, providing useful frameworks and methods for understanding convergence innovation across a range of sectors, countries and technologies. The book also demonstrates the pressing need for more in-depth research into the ways in which convergence innovation is shaping firm strategy, new technologies, infrastructures and markets. No doubt these issues will be taken up further by the authors and others in this exciting new research agenda.

In summary, this is a uniquely text rich on the convergence innovation subject, replete with evidence, theory, novelty and significant new arguments. It extends our understanding of technological convergence in promising new ways and is a very welcome and timely contribution to the broader field of innovation studies.

Michael Hobday
SPRU, Sussex University

1 Introduction

Kong-rae Lee

1. Why convergence innovation?

We have seen new innovations such as smart cars, drones, 3D printings, smart phones, nano particles, Internet of Things (IoT) and bio materials emerging almost daily. People are surprised at the amazing functions of smart phones or, alternatively, feel confused about the new jargons surrounding all the new technologies and functions. The Schumpeterian prediction (1976) that innovations will routinely emerge as results of mass R&D activities undertaken in large organizations is now socially recognized in the modern industrial world. Indeed, almost every class of business entity including small venture firms, individual entrepreneurs and medium- and large-size firms innovate by applying their particular knowledge bases. As we enter the twenty-first century, this accelerating trend of innovation promises to continue to shake up and restructure the global economy with both negative and positive outcomes for individuals, businesses and other organizations.

Some scholars have begun to call this new innovation trajectory the fourth industrial revolution: the first was water- and steam-powered mechanization; the second was electricity-based mass production; and the third industrial revolution centered on digital information and electronics technologies. The World Economic Forum (WEF) held on January 2016 in Davos, Switzerland, took *the Fourth Industrial Revolution* as a discussion agenda. While the third industrial revolution was characterized as the informatization of the global world via information and telecommunications technology, the fourth industrial revolution is characterized by a convergence of technologies, creating new categories of product such as smart cars, drones, 3D printings, nano, bio and new generations of smarter phones. The impact of the revolution on the economy and the society is expected to be far greater than that of the third industrial revolution in terms of speed and scope.

Technological innovation has been traditionally featured as having a variety of characteristics, from simple learning for imitation to complex learning for more advanced technologies. Modern innovations have had a strong tendency towards convergence in which information technology (IT) plays a central role across vast areas of industry creating a bewildering variety of new products and services. Going beyond IT, other technologies are also converging or being converged at varying degrees of speed and depth of integration, routinely generating new intellectual property right issues. The phenomenon of convergence is likely to further deepen and widen in the future due to intense competition among firms in global markets. This applies especially to manufacturing firms in the East, and South East Asian countries have been active in convergence innovation, in some respects, as we show below, leading the new global industrial revolution.

Looking back into the history of technological innovation, Rosenberg (1963, 1982) identified the phenomenon of convergence that had emerged at the end of the nineteenth century. He discovered that closely related technological problems were solved and shared among manufacturers of different types of machines. Machines confronted a similar collection of technological problems dealing with such matters as power transmission, control devices, feed mechanisms, friction reduction, and a broad array of challenges connected with the properties of metals. Although these problems became common to the production of a wide range of commodities, they were apparently unrelated from the viewpoint of the nature of the final product. Rosenberg called this phenomenon 'technological convergence' and argued that the intense specialization which developed in the second half of the nineteenth century owed its existence to combinations of technological convergence.

Almost two centuries since then, this convergence phenomenon is now flourishing in every industry and promises to shake the global economy to its core. The convergence between many user sectors and machining technology explored by Rosenberg continues. However, convergence innovations are universally arising in almost all technological fields and industrial areas (OECD, 1993; Rafols and Meyer, 2006; Roco and Bainbridge, 2002).

Convergence innovation is expected to evolve up to the point that different technologies are deeply integrated and some chemically mixed, resulting in completely new types of technologies and products in the future. As a result, firms and R&D organizations are desperately pursuing convergence in order to obtain competitive advantage. New products developed through convergence increasingly shape modern innovation processes, bringing about the fourth industrial revolution.

Surprisingly, very little research on convergence innovation has been carried out. The majority of innovation studies have centered on specific technological and industrial changes mostly conducted in the industrialized countries. However, few studies have systematically investigated the new innovations centered on convergence and their impacts on the economy and society. Innovation scholars have yet to empirically investigate convergence innovation, and, as a result, we have little in the way of conceptualization, hypothesis and theory to guide our understanding of this phenomenon. This lacuna has motivated the editor and authors of this book to investigate the issue and hopefully motivate other innovation scholars and students to research convergence innovation.

2. Conceptual guide to managing convergence innovation

2.1 *Managing processes of convergence*

The term 'convergence' here indicates primarily technological convergence and can be defined as a horizontal integration of diverse technological knowledge bases.[1] Horizontal integration means the absorption of diverse fields of knowledge for the purpose of creating new functions, products, processes and services. It often leads to a broadening of the scope of technological specialization and more diverse interactions with users.[2] This phenomenon occurred within metal processing industries and between machinery industries at the end of the nineteenth century (Rosenberg, 1963, 1982), between electronics and machineries in the 1970s (Kodama, 1986, 1994, 1991), and more recently among a variety of industries including information and communication, chemicals, foods, machine tools, and pharmaceutical industries (Lee and Hwang, 2005).

A terminology similar to convergence innovation was used in other innovation studies (Kodama, 1986, 1994, 1991; Lee, 2007; Lee, Yun and Jeong, 2015). For instance, Kodama argued that there are two fundamental types of innovation: one is the technological breakthrough, and the other is the technology fusion, which is a similar term to convergence innovation. While breakthrough innovations are associated with strong leadership in a particular technology, technology fusion is only possible with the concerted efforts of several different industries. Kodama placed particular emphasis on the latter because it contributes not only to the rapid growth of companies that make technological innovation possible but also to the gradual growth of all the companies in many industries. Kodama's paper mainly featured new trends in Japanese innovations. Our book builds on Rosenberg's and Kodama's pioneering work, expanding research into other countries and diverse industrial and business contexts and, for the first time, illustrating modern convergence innovation as the primary driver of the fourth industrial revolution.

The process of convergence needs to be better understood in order to efficiently manage its dynamics and better utilize its outputs for human beings and organizations. Convergence may be better understood by comparing its characteristics before and after the convergence episode. The overall features of convergence innovation are also likely to change during and after convergence taking place. Furthermore, the characteristics of the technical elements involved may change after convergence, whereas the complexity of products may well be reduced because some components are chemically 'melted down' or combined. Moreover, convergence may simplify the production and design processes for one generation of products but lead to more complexity and/or lock in with the next generation of products.[3] Similarly, processes of convergence may reveal a creative or a radical dimension in the character of final products.

Despite the lack of study of concerning processes of convergence, Kim (2014) recently pointed to convergence innovation between printing technology and electronic technology and argued that there is continuous disequilibrium between converging technologies, which are divided into two types: 'reference technology' and 'matching technology'. The two types of converging technologies tend to innovate at different degrees of speed generating disequilibrium between reference technology and matching technology, requiring further innovation to restore an optimal balance between the functions of the technologies. This study argues that a process of fine tuning, involving mutual matching and minute adjustments across disparate technologies, is required to achieve the performance given target. Chapter 7 of this book elaborates this explanation for the case of specialized textile machinery suppliers.

As this book shows, managing the processes of convergence innovation requires an understanding of its various dimensions not only at the technological level but also at the organization, industry and even national levels. Processes of convergence will be investigated for the case of textile machinery technology in Chapter 7, for the case of railway technology in Chapter 8, at the organizational level in Chapter 4 and at the industry and country levels in Chapter 6. These investigations are useful for supporting not only the innovation strategy of the firms concerned but also for government policy makers in charge of promoting industrial innovation.

2.2   *Managing learning, networks and communication*

As this book shows, one of the most important elements of the convergence process is learning. Managing learning processes well is crucial in the successful management of convergence innovation. The concepts of firm learning process and the building up of technological capability suggested by Bell (1984, 1995) are usefully applied to the understanding of convergence innovation.

The process of learning and convergence at individual and collective levels can be simply depicted as in Figure 1.1. Here, the processes of convergence begin as person A with a cognitive map interacts with another holding a different cognitive map (tacit knowledge B of person B). The individual observes, analogizes, discerns and behaves during the learning process during the accumulation of tacit knowledge. The person's interaction evolves into a collective learning process that causes the generation of new knowledge. The new knowledge also helps create another set of new knowledge (C) after it absorbs both codified and tacit knowledge generated by the third individual (person C) with other cognitive maps. This process involves socialization, externalization, and combination and internalization of knowledge, as hypothesized by Nonaka (1994). Given this active social interaction and learning, the diversity of application for any given technology becomes ever larger so that the convergence involved in creating new functions, products and services becomes possible.

As time goes by, collective learning becomes more important for convergence. On the one hand, research and development teams as collective agents learn new technological knowledge during one time period and create new functions, products, processes or services through the convergence of different technologies. This may involve incremental or a radical innovation. Well-functioning networks

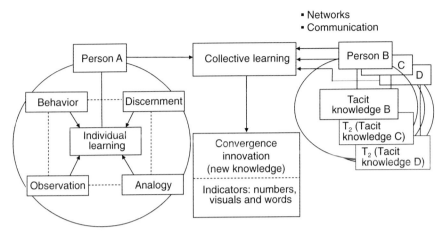

Figure 1.1 A conceptualization of convergence processes at the individual level

and communications are important mechanisms in the effective learning required to support convergence innovation. The networks linked to convergence are investigated in the third chapter of the book, and many types of technological learning at the firm level are identified in the second chapter, highlighting their importance in convergence innovation.

On the other hand, convergence has a feature of a life cycle like any other innovation process. It begins as researchers begin socialization activities in a research network and learn knowledge. Then, an innovation emerges as the researchers generate new knowledge that becomes the source of new functions, products, processes or services. Creative knowledge eventually becomes routine as the researchers and engineers move towards a stabilization stage that completes the life cycle of convergence. New technology created in the process of convergence innovation becomes embodied in the cognitive map of a group or an organization that is the result of collective learning activities.

Collective learning is a distinctive feature of convergence, which includes the acquisition, assimilation, integration and creation of knowledge. Social interaction is a bridge for convergence between diverse groups of people with different cognitive maps. Collective agents learn new knowledge as past knowledge becomes obsolete. Collective learning ensures the creation of new knowledge or technology through convergence innovation as with processes at the individual level.

Organizations, especially firms, get involved in the convergence process, and whether they manage the process well or not may determine the success or failure of not only their innovative activities but also their entire business. Successful firms achieve multi-product diversification through the active integration of diverse technologies. Managing convergence at the firm level is primarily a function of the creation of conditions under which learning opportunities emerge and are exploited (Tidd, Bessant and Pavitt, 2001). Large-size firms may have the capability to pursue convergence innovation based on their large scope of knowledge embodied in their R&D centers (Teece, 1976). By contrast, small- and medium-sized firms may have more limited opportunities but, in some cases, can be more focused and flexible than large firms.

Managing convergence innovation at the firm level is emphasized in the fourth chapter of this book. Four areas of management are identified to reveal the core processes: product, process, personnel and information infrastructure. The chapter introduces four stages in how to successfully manage convergence processes, which inevitably requires changes in culture, value, behavior, institutions and even the mindset of employees, especially in locked-in organizations: de-freezing, organizing, implementing and freezing (Yun and Kim, 2016). The authors argue that existing ideas and institutions should be de-freezed in order to adopt new ones. At the same time, organizing new directions and targets incorporating new ideas and implementing them effectively should be followed. After everything is set up well, a freezing stage will be necessary to achieve a new phase of stability.

2.3 *Managing convergence at the meso and the country levels*

To manage convergence innovation at the meso and the country levels calls for innovation policies designed to accelerate convergence at the industry, regional or country level. How best to formulate innovation policies depends upon the appropriate policy targets. Policy makers need to understand the principles of convergence and how to best apply them in their situations in order to effectively manage and generate convergence innovation. In this regard, the chapters of this book provide guidelines to assist with making policies to promote convergence innovation at the meso and country levels.

Innovation policies to promote convergence are not likely to be different markedly from traditional innovation policies. As Schumpeter (1976) predicted, there is an innate nature to innovation trajectories, and presumably convergence innovation is no different. The various professionals involved play concerted roles in creating the emerging technologies. Engineers and businessmen in the same and different fields socially interact, perform learning activities and thereby create new technologies and new industries based on convergence innovation.

As this book demonstrates, the nature and degree of convergence innovation varies by industry. The diversity of application areas of any given set of technology in an industry tends to be sufficiently large to further create new products, processes or services. Each industry reveals a unique mode of knowledge collaboration between different people and varied sets of ideas. Each industry presents a different profile of customers, ideas and knowledge of users and suppliers, as well as divergent market demands for innovation. The collaborative mode created and knowledge sources utilized triggers diversity in convergence innovation. The ability to utilize diverse knowledge sources strategically enables particular firms to lead convergence innovation thereby gaining a unique advantage in the global marketplace.

Inter-industry diversity is also reflected in cross-country differences in convergence innovation. The country level analyses in this book show that managing the convergence capability of a country is associated with the degree of its innovation. Chapter 6 deals with this issue by providing empirical examinations of the degree of convergence innovations in four countries: China, Japan, South Korea and Taiwan. Intriguingly, the results of the analysis show a degree of synchronization in the trend of convergence across four countries.

3.   Contents and objectives of the book

This book is composed of three main parts with closely related aims and objectives. The overall aim of the book is to show the nature, origins, extent and impact of convergence innovation, focusing on the case of East and South East Asia. The book also develops the conceptualization and theoretical basis needed to understand convergence innovation and the firm and government level policy implications that flow from convergence innovation. The objective of Part I, made up of two chapters, is to show how individuals and firms learn and diffuse knowledge, revealing the primary origins and carriers of convergence innovation. Chapter 2 identifies new modes of convergence learning and shows how they have evolved one after another. The chapter describes how technological learning has gone beyond the simple mode of learning-by-doing, producing forms such as learning-by-porting, learning-by-using and learning-by-integration, essential to convergence innovation.

The objective of Chapter 3 is to uncover the nature of the convergence innovation process revealing, for example, how innovations such as new products, practices and ideas are created and then diffused throughout organizations and society. Adopting a network analytic perspective, the chapter begins by describing the underlying network paradigm. It then discusses the various network models involved in the cognitive processes by which individuals generate innovations, including neural networks, spatial and graphical theoretic models. The chapter goes on to analyze individual (ego-centric), social and information networks and their implications for the creative processes central to convergence innovation.

The objective of the two chapters of Part II is to show how firms, industries and countries are able to navigate and manage the processes of convergence innovation. Chapter 4 focuses on the processes of convergence in the management of large firms, taking the example of Samsung Electronics of South Korea. While convergence innovation brings many rewards, it also introduces hardships and obstacles that must be overcome. The chapter provides information on how to cope with the anxiety that changes brought about by convergence innovation causes and shows how the firm utilizes objectives and visions for implementing necessary strategic and operational changes.

Chapter 5 deals with the importance of diversity in navigating convergence innovation at the meso and country levels. The chapter argues that diversity and non-conformity are characteristics of the individuals and teams that constitute convergence innovation, requiring a space of creative freedom. It proposes, in the context of Asian countries, a transformational change for growing out of the heritage of the catch-up competitiveness agenda and for diversification to be an important part of science and technology policy.

Part III, made up of three chapters, deals with cases of convergence innovation in Asian industries and countries. Chapter 6 concerns intra- and inter-industry convergence, in which five industry types are grouped based on their innovation characteristics: science based; scale-intensive; specialized suppliers; supplier dominated; and information intensive (Pavitt, 1984). The chapter also presents results on inter-industry convergence.

Chapter 7 investigates convergence innovation in specialized textile machinery suppliers in South Korea. It shows that the degree of convergence innovation has continuously increased over the period of 2001–2011, shaped by two types of innovators: outside-in and inside-out convergence. The former was active in textile machinery suppliers as they utilize their core competence for exploiting business opportunities in other machines, while the latter was active when the textile machinery industry was in a boom period, as specialized suppliers integrated outside technologies in order to solve their technological problems.

Chapter 8 links convergence innovation to city innovation systems in which a path for convergence has been created. The cases of Kuala Lumpur and Cyberjaya of Malaysia show how a railway company in Malaysia pursues and assimilates rail technology to attain capability in operation and maintenance technology, through the first decade of the twenty-first century. The analysis presents the knowledge ties that enabled the emergence of convergence innovation in the two city clusters.

The last chapter presents conclusions and policy implications. Policy implications to promote convergence innovation are drawn from seven perspectives: spatial, process, user-supplier, R&D, human side, institutional and cultural. These implications suggest useful insights for local and central governments who are pursuing convergence innovation for economic growth and social welfare improvement.

Notes

1 The term 'horizontal integration' in this book contrasts with that put forward by Teece (1976), who is concerned with organizational integration over value chains.
2 Iansiti (1998) argues that technology integration is made up of the set of problem-solving activities that are performed to match a new element of technical knowledge to the complex architecture of established competences.
3 Complexity is often determined by the nature/simplicity of the interfaces between components and also the prior knowledge of the firm. What has been done many times by one firm appears very simple to it but might be extremely complex for another firm with little experience.

References

Bell, M. (1984), "Learning and the accumulation of industrial technological capacity in developing countries", in M. Fransman, and K. King (eds.), *Technological Capability in the Third World*, pp. 187–209, London: Macmillan.
Bell, M. and Pavitt, K. (1995), "The development of technological capabilities", in I. Hague (ed.), *Trade, Technology and Industrial Competitiveness*, pp. 69–101, Washington: World Bank.

Iansiti, M. (1998), *Technology Integration*, Boston: Harvard Business School Press.

Kim, E. (2014), *Evolutionary Patterns and Dynamics of Technological Convergence: The Case of Printed Electronics*, Ph.D. Dissertation, Daejeon: KAIST.

Kodama, F. (1986), "Inter-disciplinary research: Japanese innovation in mechatronics technology", *Science and Public Policy*, vol. 13, no. 1, pp. 44–51.

Kodama, F. (1991), *Analyzing Japanese High Technologies: The Techno Paradigm Shift*, London: Pinter Publishers.

Kodama, F. (1994), *Emerging Patterns of Innovation*, Boston: Harvard University Press.

Lee, K.-R. (2007), "Patterns and processes of contemporary technology fusion: The case of intelligent robots", *Asian Journal of Technology Innovation*, vol. 15, no. 2, pp. 45–65.

Lee, K.-R. and Hwang, J.-T. (2005), *A Study on Innovation System with Multi-Technology Fusion* (in Korean), Seoul: STEPI Policy Study 2005–17.

Lee, K.-R., Yun, J. J. and Jeong, E.-S. (2015), "Convergence innovation of the textile machinery industry in Korea", *Asian Journal of Technology Innovation*, vol. 23, no. s.1, pp. 58–73.

Nonaka, I. (1994), "A dynamic theory of organizational knowledge creation", *Organizational Science*, vol. 5, no. 1, pp. 14–37.

OECD (1993), *Technology Fusion: A Path to Innovation, the Case of Optoelectronics*, Paris: OECD.

Pavitt, K. (1984), "Sectoral patterns of technical change: Towards a taxonomy and a theory", *Research Policy*, vol. 13, no. 6, pp. 343–373.

Rafols, I. and Meyer, M. (2006), *Knowledge-Sourcing Strategies for Cross-Disciplinarity in Bionanotechnology*, Brighton: SPRU Electronic Working Paper Series: 152.

Roco, M. C. and Bainbridge, W. S. (2002), *Converging Technologies for Improving Human Performance*, Arlington, VA: NSF.

Rosenberg, N. (1963), "Technological change in the machine tool industry, 1840–1910", *Journal of Economic History*, vol. 23, no. 4, pp. 414–446.

Rosenberg, N. (1982), *Inside the Black Box: Technology and Economics*, Cambridge: Cambridge University Press.

Schumpeter, J. A. (1976), *Capitalism, Socialism and Democracy*, London: George Allen & Unwin.

Teece, D. J. (1976), *Vertical Integration and Vertical Divestiture in the US Petroleum Industry*, Stanford Institute for Energy Studies.

Tidd, J., Bessant, J. and Pavitt, K. (2001) (2nd ed.), *Managing Innovation-Integrating Technological, Market and Organizational Change*, Chischester: Wiley.

Yun, J.-Y. and Kim, C. (2016), "Convergence innovation in the management of large firms: Samsung electronics", in Lee Kong-rae (ed.), *Managing Convergence Innovation*, pp. 68–85, London: Routledge.

Part I

How firms learn and diffuse

2 Changes in modes of technological learning

Fumio Kodama, Yukihiko Nakata, and Tamotsu Shibata

1. Introduction

It is argued that the process of convergence innovation is a continuous disequilibrium between reference technology and its matching technology, which adjusts optimal balance between the functions of the two technologies. The process of convergence innovation is also featured as a *learning* process that requires both vertical and horizontal convergence.

In this context, our arguments in this chapter are based on the premise that the innovation process can be best formulated as a *learning* process by society. As is well known, the existence of "learning-by-doing" was first emphasized by K. J. Arrow (1962) in his article "The Economic Implications of Learning by Doing." This is a form of learning that takes place at the manufacturing stage after a product has been designed. Learning at this stage consists of developing increasing skills in production. This has the effect of reducing real labor costs per unit of production.

Using the accumulated production units as an indicator of skills gained, we can measure empirically the process of learning-by-doing. In other words, the phenomena of learning-by-doing can be graphically demonstrated in the form of the "learning curve," with the real unit price in the Y-coordinate and the *accumulated* production units in the X-coordinate; thus, the *monotone decreasing* curve in this graphical representation gives evidence of learning-by-doing. Based on these measurements, for example, it is widely accepted that the cost of labor decreases by 20–30 percent as the accumulated production *doubles*. One of the well-known studies includes airframe production and shipbuilding in the US industries. In more recent studies using microelectronics, it has become a normal practice to use the *logarithmic* scale in both of the coordinates, because of the dramatic progress in productivity that has occurred. Many authors demonstrated that the learning curve of integrated circuits represents an obvious decreasing curve *even* in this scale of logarithmic coordinates (Noyce, 1979).

Furthermore, we would like to refer to the studies by business school scholars. Abernathy (1974) had drawn the learning curve observed in the early period of over one hundred years' progress in automobiles. From the viewpoint of strategy formulation, Porter (1979) discussed the "experience curve" as a key element of industry structure in many manufacturing industries as well as in some service industries. Rather than the better-known learning curve, which refers to the efficiency achieved over a period of time by workers through *repetitive* work, Porter argues that the experience curve encompasses many factors apart from the learning curve, as the causes of the decrease in unit costs are also due to other factors such as economies of scale, and capital-labor substitution.

However, ever since such studies had been made, several changes related to the technological learning phenomena have occurred, such as the global shift in technological leaderships, emergence of new sciences (e.g., bio-technologies and computer sciences), and deepening of systemic innovations. In parallel with these technological advancements, new modes of learning emerged one after another. And these modes are different from the mode of learning-by-doing. In this paper, we describe how technological learning has gone beyond the simple mode of learning-by-doing.

2.   Learning-by-using

When it comes to those industries characterized by a high degree of systemic complexity, learning-by-doing becomes a very *subtle* process. In this context, Rosenberg (1982) proposed a clear distinction between "learning-by-doing" and "learning-by-using." He argues that one of the basic purposes of the learning-by-using process is to determine the optimal *performance* characteristics of a durable *capital good* as they affect the length of useful *life*.

We argue that those practices often described as uniquely Japanese – such as close collaboration between manufacturers and suppliers, high degree of attention paid to product integrity, and management style based on consensus building – can be better explained by learning-by-using rather than learning-by-doing. This is a new way of looking at the sources of Japanese competitiveness, which had so far been explained by narrowly defined phrases such as quality control circle activities and just-in-time production. These are all related to learning-by-doing, but a more broadly defined Japanese competitiveness can only be analyzed by means of learning-by-using.

We have tried to validate the hypothesis that the former USSR system could not accommodate the mode of learning-by-using,[1] by investigating the "continuous casting technology" production method. It had been widely believed that the USSR was far ahead of Western countries in applying the continuous casting technology method. It was reported that during the 1952–1962 period, the USSR had put as many as eight strands of equipment into operation when there existed only fourteen strands in operation worldwide during this period (Japan Steel Association, 1996). Thereafter, the situation changed drastically. The diffusion curves in Japan, the United Kingdom, West Germany, and the USSR depicted in Figure 2.1 make it obvious that the USSR was left far behind other countries in its diffusion rate. It also shows that Japan achieved the highest rate in the 1970s, even though it started its technology development only after the 1960s.

In the 1970s, Japan imported technology from several countries including the USSR and rushed into constructing many plants, even making *wider slabs* of

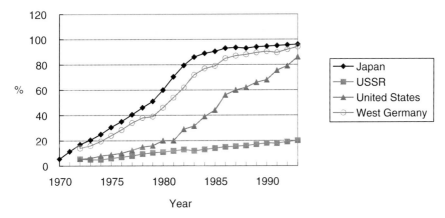

Figure 2.1 International comparison in diffusion of continuous casting production
Source: Nippon Steel Corp.

steel by developing new production techniques matching continuous casting and large-scale *revolving furnace technologies*. Thus, Japan took a leadership position in this technology. The annual diffusion rate of continuous casting, measured by the percentage of steel produced through continuous casting to total steel production, surpassed *50 percent* of that in 1979, and attained over 90 percent in 1985. This Japanese technology was exported to Western countries, which achieved a diffusion rate around 80 percent in the 1990s, while the diffusion rate in the USSR remained as low as 20 percent even in 1990, as is clearly shown in the figure depicted above.

Why did the USSR face such setbacks, despite having developed several component technologies[2] such as the mold vibration mechanism? The key to solve this puzzle is that what is needed for a stable and sustainable operation of continuous casting is not the fragmented collection of components technologies but the computer technology which integrates these components into a total system of continuous casting (Kodama et al., 1998). In other words, it was information technology that enabled continuous casting, as shown vividly in Figure 2.2, which compares the system of 1962 with that of 1992.

Indeed, as clearly shown in this figure, there had been only *four* primitive types of measurement in the continuous casting system of 1962, while in the 1992 system we find as many as *eight* different types of measurements using *computers* which perform such tasks as process control, command control, operations management, quality control, equipment maintenance, and collection of performance data. In addition to these subsystem computers, the whole process control of continuous casting is monitored and controlled by a central on-line computer by coordinating the subsystem computers.

While the concept of learning-by-using may explain why the USSR experienced setbacks in steel-making, it does not provide us with a sufficient reason why Japan became the most efficient steel-maker in the world. According to

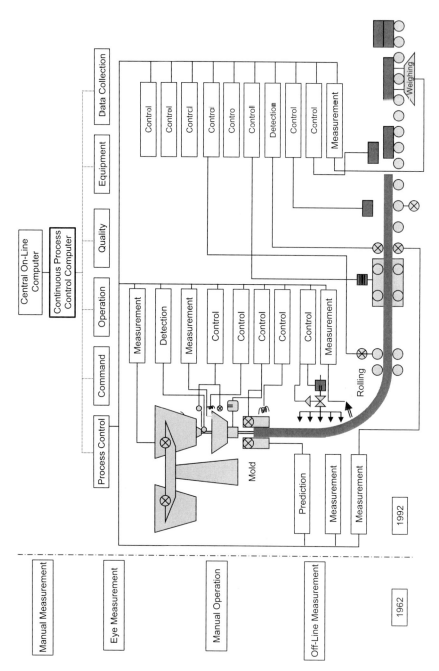

Figure 2.2 Computerization in continuous casting from 1962 to 1992

Source: Nippon Steel Corporation

Rosenberg (1984), the learning-by-using experience generates two very different kinds of useful knowledge that we may designate as *embodied* or *disembodied*. As far as the embodied knowledge is concerned, the early experience with a new technology leads to better understanding of the relationship between specific design characteristics and performance that permit subsequent improvements in design. Out of this confluence comes a steady flow of small improvements that can be *embodied* in new hardware.

Such an argument leads us to pay attention to relationships between the steel manufacturers and equipment suppliers. In the case of steel-making, we investigated the relationship between steel-makers and heavy-machinery suppliers. The empirical evidence of joint development efforts between those two industries can be ascertained from the number of their *joint patent* applications. By using the patent retrieval system developed by the Nippon Steel Corporation, we compiled the number of joint patent applications for the period 1977 to 1993, which is further classified into *four* technical areas: iron-making, steel-making, rolling, and surface treatment, as depicted in Table 2.1. On *average* for all the four technical areas of steel-making processes (see column A in the table), 17 percent of patent applications had been in the form of joint applications. This figure is lower than the average for the technique of *surface treatment*, where only a few technically sophisticated suppliers exist. Thus most technologies are developed solely by the steel producers themselves.

Since we are interested in the technical knowledge "embodied" in the new designs of manufacturing equipment, therefore, we have to *single out* those joint patent applications between steel manufacturers and *heavy machinery* suppliers (see column B in the table). The *thirteen* largest companies are identified,[3] and the percentage of joint application with these companies is determined. The share of these applications with heavy machinery suppliers in the total joint application is calculated as depicted in the last column (B/A) of Table 2.1. As much as 30–40 percent of all the joint applications are conducted with heavy machinery suppliers in the areas of *steel-making* and *metal-rolling*, while the research into component technologies of iron-making and surface treatment are mostly done by the steel companies themselves – that is, about 10 percent as seen in the table. When it comes to metal rolling, the argument of embodiment becomes obvious, because the steel companies purchase equipment from the heavy machinery

Table 2.1 Joint patent application by Nippon Steel Co. (1977–1993)

Process	Overall joint application ratio (A)	Ratio of joint application with heavy machinery suppliers (B)	(B/A)
Iron making	17.22%	1.73%	10.01%
Steel making	21.04%	6.36%	30.23%
Metal rolling	18.19%	6.85%	37.66%
Surface treatment	15.49%	1.86%	12.01%

suppliers and much of knowledge created by steel producers in terms of optimal operation of rolling mills is embodied in the form of design modifications made by heavy machinery suppliers.

As described above, learning-by-using includes both embodied and disembodied knowledge. As far as the disembodied knowledge is concerned, the knowledge generated leads to certain alternations in use that require no modifications in hardware design. Prolonged experience with the hardware design reveals information about performance and operating characteristics that, in turn, leads to new practices that increase the productivity of the hardware (Rosenberg, 1982). In several studies on knowledge creation, there exists a widely held dichotomy between *tacit* and *explicit* knowledge. Tacit knowledge includes practices and skills, and thus cannot be embodied in hardware design. Bateson (1973) associates tacit knowledge with *analog* information and explicit knowledge with *digital* information. If this one-to-one correspondence is valid, the computerization of manufacturing processes is changing the dichotomy between tacit and explicit knowledge, because computerization is not possible without digital transformation of the analog data – that is, the tacit knowledge. This hypothesis can be tested by investigating how the manufacturing process of steel-making had been computerized, because it is well known that the operation of the blast furnace involves a high degree of skill – that is, tacit knowledge – developed and owned by line workers at factories. In Figure 2.3, therefore, we compare the computerization of blast furnaces in 1962 with that in 1992.

This figure shows how and where a lot of information is collected through many inserted censors, how the collected information is processed using various *control modeling* based on scientific knowledge in physics and chemistry, and how the *artificial intelligence* (AI) program is constructed upon the knowledge gained through experiences in operation, most of which are *tacit* knowledge. All the features described above appear only in the right half of the picture that depicts the computerization in 1992, while the left half of the picture shows only four censors inserted (furnace top gas analyzer, feed material level meter, shaft temperature gauge, and furnace bottom temperature gauge) in the 1962 system. This picture illustrates that most tacit knowledge has been *transformed* into explicit knowledge through computerization of the steel-making operations.

Nonaka (1990) used the expression "articulation" for the transformation from tacit knowledge into explicit knowledge, and "internalization" from explicit to tacit knowledge. As for the transformation from tacit to explicit knowledge, however, we suggest a better expression, based on our detailed investigation into how this transformation took place in the Japanese steel industry (Kodama, 1999). The Western practice of transforming tacit knowledge to explicit knowledge is through external computer programmers who conduct a series of careful interviews with factory skilled workers and then transform the collected information into computer programs. On the contrary, in Japan, the companies taught skilled factory workers computer programming and then encouraged them to transform their tacit knowledge into computer programs themselves (Tomiura, 1997). The Japanese practice of codifying tacit knowledge is therefore very different from

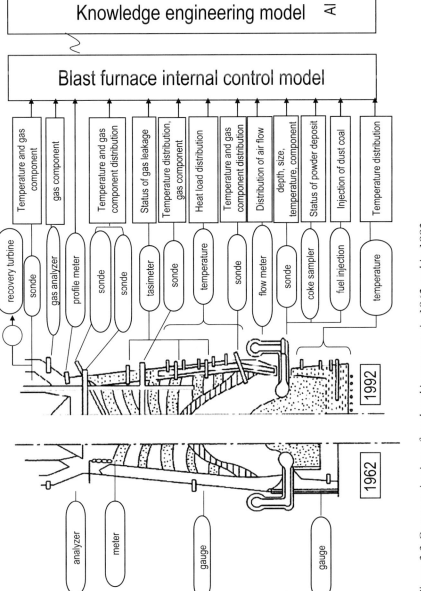

Figure 2.3 Computerization of steel-making process in 1962 and in 1992

Source: created by Nippon Steel Corp.

the conventional method employed in the Western industries. Therefore, I would suggest that it is more appropriate to use the expression "externalization" for the transformation from tacit to explicit knowledge.

In summary, the disembodied knowledge was *externalized* into explicit knowledge in the form of computer software. The effectiveness of the dichotomy between embodied and disembodied, therefore, gets less valid when we consider the ongoing process of computerizing tacit knowledge, because this category of knowledge is after all embodied in a software product. Indeed, recent developments in information technology are making this distinction less plausible. Thus, production processes of the steel-making industry have been innovated by integrating computer technology and increased its production capacity and productivity. In hindsight, this is a convergence innovation (in *embryonic*) between conventional steel-making technology and computer technology.

At this stage of steel-making technology development, both tacit and explicit knowledge had been finally *embodied* in the *capital goods* (e.g., manufacturing equipment and machinery, and installed computer software packages). We can easily imagine, therefore, how rapid technology transfer can be made across national boundaries, at least as far as the steel industry is concerned. The unprecedented speed of catching-up realized during 1975–1985 by the Korean steel industry (i.e., POSCO) is clearly demonstrated in Figure 2.4. Indeed, this case alludes that we have gone far beyond the simple notion of learning-by-using, which we will describe in the next section.

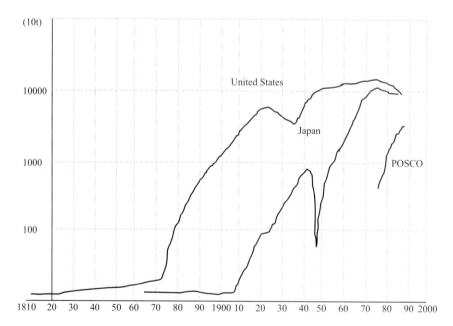

Figure 2.4 Historical trends of crude steel production in the US, Japan, and Korea
Source: Sato (1996)

3. Learning-by-integration

Going beyond learning-by-using, we will now move to another different *category* of learning. Linsu Kim (1997) studied the types of transfer channels used by the Korean industry in the period from 1962 to 1993. He classified the transfer channels into *three* categories: foreign direct investment (FDI); technological licensing; and purchase of capital goods.

His investigation reveals that the Korean industry relied heavily on the *third* channel – that is, purchasing technologically sophisticated capital goods. The Korean industry purchased as much as $278.8 billion worth of capital goods from advanced countries, while the amount of FDI into Korea was $11.2 billion, and they paid $7.9 billion for technology licensing. According to Kim, the figure for the *third* channel (purchasing capital goods) is relatively much higher than those for the first (FDI) and the second (licensing) channels, in comparison with countries such as Argentina, Brazil, India, and Mexico.

Kim further investigated from which country the Korean industry mostly imported its capital goods. He found that the United States and Japan together made up almost 70–80 percent of the total amount in each of the three channels during the twenty-year period from 1960 to 1980. When it comes to each individual channel of technology transfer, however, Japan differs from the United States as far as Korean importation of technology is concerned. For the purchase of capital goods, 43 percent of total purchase comes from Japan and 26 percent from the United States; while 48 percent of all technological licensing comes from the United States and 32 percent from Japan; and 40 percent of all FDI is made by Japan and 30 percent by the United States. By relying on the transfer channel of purchasing technologically sophisticated capital goods, the Korean industry procured selectively all the goods for production ranging from manufacturing equipment and functional parts to computer software products from all over the world, and *integrated* them into their productive capacities, which made them the most efficient in the world. This process of integration is definitely not *automatic*. Without comprehending the characteristics of each individual component and the interactive relationships among them, it could not have been possible for the Korean industry to succeed in building the most efficient production system in the world. Therefore, I will call this method of learning "learning-by-integration."

It is equally true that Korea made every effort to develop the human resources necessary for accommodating this type of learning-by-integration. This is especially true for developing scientific and engineering talents. Many Korean young talents were educated, very often up to the PhD degree, in advanced countries particularly in the United States. They gained working experience as engineers and professors in these countries and came back to Korea when its economy took off as a technologically advanced society exporting many high-technology products to the world market.[4]

When it comes to high-technology, however, the concept of learning-by-integration becomes more *complex*. One of the most conspicuous elements of high-tech development has been the "co-development" of product and process technologies.[5] The development of a product is conducted *concurrently* with the development of its production technology (Kodama, 1995). In this context, learning-by-integration in high technologies implies that process technology development should be *integrated* into the product technology development process. Without opportunities to accumulate production experience, high-tech development is not possible. This implies that a *localized* technical knowledge is developed and applied to less demanding, low-end markets *first*. As the technology is mastered and production experiences accumulated, development is directed toward the high-end market. Branscomb (1989) once characterized the approach taken by Japanese consumer electronics firms to the commercialization of new technology as a "trickle-up" strategy: a new technology is introduced in a consumer item rather than a high-end or industrial product in order to *gain* manufacturing experience at *low* functional levels and at low cost. At the same time, studies are conducted on functions that are necessary for products in higher-value markets. Only after the process and the technology are mastered is the technology introduced into markets with higher margins and more specialized applications.

A review of the development of *liquid crystal display* in the electronics industry will show that the trickle-up strategy comes from the process of perfecting earlier scientific findings. Although Europeans discovered liquid crystals almost a century ago, the basic idea of using them in display devices came about only when RCA (Radio Corporation of America) invented the dynamic scattering mode in 1967. At the time RCA was trying to commercialize liquid crystals, however, the standard for display technology was the cathode-ray tube (CRT). A *flat panel* display was nothing more than a *dream*, and other technological alternatives to liquid crystals existed, including electroluminescence and plasma display. RCA had regarded liquid crystal technology as a display method for *general* purposes. Thus, RCA chose to stick with CRT technology, as did most manufacturers of CRT screens.

There were, however, clear commercial applications for *flat panel* display, and the correct technological choice was made by more specialized manufacturers with technology goals suitable to such applications. Sharp Corporation, for example, was caught up in a stiff competition in the development of *pocket calculators*. The company recognized the key to success lay in creating smaller, *thinner* products that used minimal energy. Thereafter, Sharp Corporation gradually expanded its application of LCD technologies as various innovations followed, bringing larger screens, greater precision, quicker responses, color displays, and greater *legibility*. Indeed, Sharp quite successfully *navigated* the trickle-up process including a shift from the *duty* drive to the *active matrix* drive, as indicated in Sharp's development and marketing history in Figure 2.5.

Having navigated the process skillfully, Sharp Corporation became one of the world's largest leading consumer-product manufacturers, holding a major position in TV sets, calculators, solar cells, and thin-film transistor LCD flat panel displays. From the standpoint of the company's history illustrated in Figure 2.5, the use of LCD for flat panel display for *television* sets might have been the *final* target in terms of the trickle-up process. Indeed, Sharp had been leading the process of applying LCD into the flat panel television sets, and had been quite successful in the early stages of this application. However, Korea and Taiwan entered into the

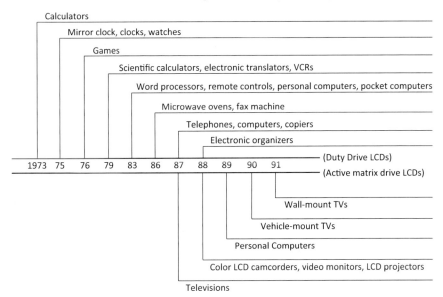

Figure 2.5 Development and marketing history of Sharp LCD products (1973–1991)
Source: Sharp Technical Report Vol.1, 1991, pp. 66–67

LCD business around 2000. After that, global leadership of LCD manufacturing shifted from Japan to Korea and Taiwan as shown in Figure 2.6.

Nevertheless, Sharp continued to invest in LCD and established the Kameyama plant in 2004 for a vertical integration of the LCD panel and LCD television. There existed several cases of co-developments among equipment-vendors and material-suppliers in the LCD production lines of the Kameyama plant. To understand how Sharp Corporation navigated the process of co-development of product and process technologies, Nakata (2005, 2009) drew *two types* of experience curves: one is related to the product, and the other to the *process*.

The experience curve of the product is based on the fact that the LCD panel size itself does matter because it can display large images. If the *glass substrate* is enlarged, larger LCD panels can be obtained; this would strengthen the product's competitiveness in the market. Therefore, LCD manufacturers competed with each other and used larger glass substrates to make larger LCD panels. Figure 2.7 shows the *experience curve* for product, showing how rapidly the glass substrate size (measured by m²) was expanded as the experience of LCD production accumulated (measured by the total area of *accumulated* production: m² base). The production of Sharp's LCD took place through coordination among LCD manufacturers, equipment-venders, and material-venders worldwide. Therefore, *global* accumulated volume of LCD production was plotted in the X-coordinate.

As shown clearly in the figure, the glass substrate area rapidly increased. The glass substrate area *doubled* approximately every 2.5 years – while the accumulated LCD production *quadrupled*. At the Sharp Corporation's Kameyama

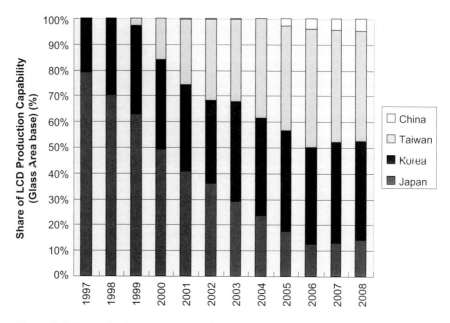

Figure 2.6 Share of LCD production capability

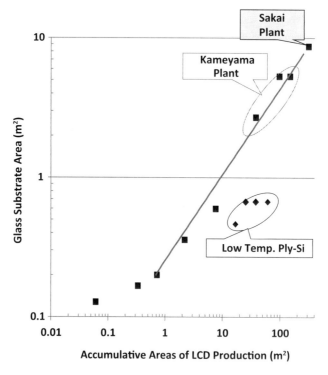

Figure 2.7 Experience curve of glass substrate size

Source: Estimated from Nikkei Micro-devices (2007) and Sharp news release

plant, the sixth-generation LCD production line was installed in January 2004, and the eighth-generation LCD line in August 2006.

In the *Sakai* plant, the tenth-generation LCD (world's largest size) production line has been in operation since October 2009. As observed from the product experience curve depicted in the figure above, the decision to invest in the tenth-generation product appears to be appropriately timed. At the time the Sakai plant went into operation, however, Sharp Corporation might not have successfully navigated the *simultaneous co-development* of product and process technologies. In order to analyze the progress of matching between product and process technologies, the investment cost per glass substrate area for each production line of each Sharp plant was calculated as shown in Figure 2.8.

As shown in the figure, the investment cost per glass substrate area was drastically reduced to one-tenth in twelve years from 1995 to 2007, as the global accumulated LCD production increased by more than one hundred times. In the case of the Sakai plant, however, the investment cost per glass substrate area did not decrease. Instead, it actually *increased* up to double that of the Kameyama plant. This indicates that over-investment could have occurred at the

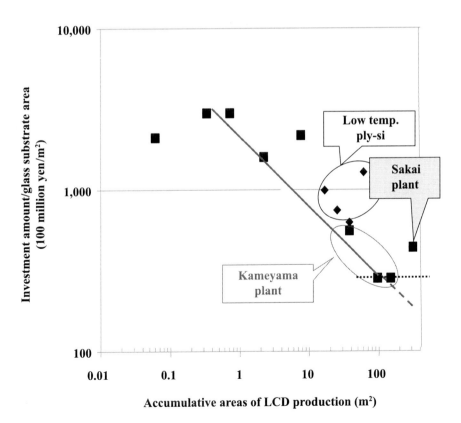

Figure 2.8 Experience curve in the investment cost per glass substrate area
Source: Nakata (2005)

Sakai plant – that is, large investment *without* process innovation. This means that Sharp was not successful in navigating the trickle-up process – that is, the simultaneous co-development of product and process technologies. In retrospect, the achievement of Sharp Corporation was far short of an ideal type of learning-by-integration when they built the Sakai plant.

4.   Upward reflection in experience curve

Abernathy (1974) had also demonstrated that the experience curve did not continue indefinitely at Ford, and that it governed only the Model T era. He argues Ford abandoned it for a performance-maximizing strategy by which the company tried to improve performance year by year at an ever higher product price. The product was the Model A.

In fact, Abernathy at *Harvard Business Review* (1974) drew the curves for average prices of the Ford line for some sixty years in an experience-curve format. He could successfully demonstrate that these prices changed concurrently, whether price is defined on a per-vehicle basis or on a per-pound basis. This comparison of the two trend lines in different periods is revealing. After the Model T was discontinued in 1927, Ford raised the price of its car from year to year. The increases were due mainly to design changes which were made to enhance comfort, performance, and safety, but which required more expensive materials and caused the price per pound to rise steadily.

Whenever a major change occurs, such as an upward reflection in experience curve as measured at Ford's learning curve, can this be generalized in other industries? In the period of more than a quarter century since 1982, the Japanese production of machine tools kept its top position in the world, as depicted below in Figure 2.9. It is to be contrasted with the Japanese electronics industry, including the LCD industry, which spectacularly emerged as the world top player in the late 1980s, but whose dominance in the world market was short-lived in retrospect. Therefore, I would argue, the Japanese machine tool industry might have overcome several major changes in its long sustained dominance.

When it comes to the thirty-five-year history of numerically controlled machine tool (NC) systems, indeed, the most epochal elemental technology was the microprocessor unit (MPU). The turning point for the adoption of MPUs was the switch from an NC system centered on hard-wired technology to an NC system centered on the MPU – that is, the switch to a soft-wired system. At that time, the knowledge and expertise accumulated in the hard-wired NC era became redundant, so we can speculate that technical issues or challenges in architecture design arose immediately after the introduction of the MPU. Shibata (2005) tried to confirm whether or not there was a change to an integral architecture just after the introduction of the MPU, by verifying whether or not the introduction of the MPU did create technical issues in NC architecture design; and if it did so, what kinds of technical issues were created.

Fanuc had already been able to secure a high market share with hard-wired modules, aggressively taking on subsequent advances in semiconductor technology. In

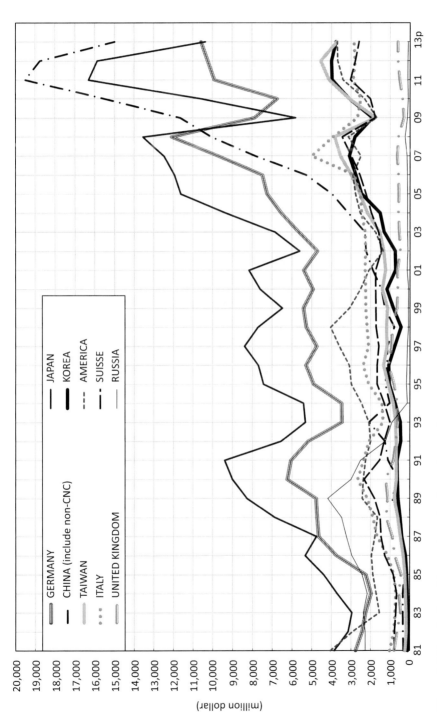

Figure 2.9 Trend of machine tool production volume of major countries

addition, Fanuc was still successful in developing the first NC system in the world to incorporate an MPU: the Fanuc 2000C system. If the existing architecture can basically be used, however, the adoption of the epoch-making elemental technology should be directly linked to a reduction in product system size. This is because if the new elemental technology can be incorporated into one of the subsystems that constitute the existing architecture, then a reduction in the size of the entire system can be achieved (Henderson and Clark, 1990). By observing the size of the NC system, we can probably infer whether or not major technical issues were created in the architecture design when the MPU was introduced.[6] The degree of system miniaturization should be sensitive to effects resulting from the presence of technical issues related to architecture design. If a temporary increase in system size is observed at that time, therefore, it is reasonable to say that technical problems concerning architecture design existed at this point of time.

On the basis of the above discussion, we will now look at the changes in the size of NC systems resulting from the adoption of a new elemental technology. Table 2.2 shows the relative surface areas for the main printed circuit boards

Table 2.2 Relative surface areas of main printed circuit boards of NC

NC system name	Start of sales	Surface area of NC printed wiring board	Main new elemental technology and characteristics
FANUC 220	1962	60.2	Transistor
FANUC 260	1966	7.5	Complete conversion to integrated circuits; subsequently, improvement and modularization in 1969
FANUC 200A	1972	Not measured	Built-in dedicated NC minicomputer; functionality could be changed by replacing software
FANUC 2000C	1975	9.5	First incorporation of a microprocessor
FANUC SYSTEM 6	1979	4.6	Adoption of custom LSI; adoption of bubble memory
FANUC Series 0	1985	2.7	Large-scale custom LSI
FANUC Series 15	1987	Not measured	Surface mounting, 32-bit bus
FANUC Series 16	1991	1.5	Three-dimensional mounting on electronic component printed circuit board
FANUC Series 16i	1997	1.0	Integration of NC control unit with LCD

Notes: The values for the printed wiring board surface are proportional to the value for the i-series of 1997. It should be also noted that the main printed circuit boards of the computation unit is not related to the motor driving function, and that Table 2.2 thus excludes newly adopted technologies in the drive unit such as the closed-loop system that was developed in 1975.

Source: Shibata, Yano and Kodama (2005)

(formerly termed printed wiring boards) of computation units for the main NC systems as well as the new elemental technologies that were incorporated into the main boards from 1962 to 1997.

That data is presented in graph form in Figure 2.10. From Table 2.2 and Figure 2.10, it is clear that in the technological development of the NC system over this thirty-five-year period, there is only one instance in which the printed circuit board surface area increased, and that was when the MPU was introduced for the first time.

The Fanuc 2000C printed circuit board, in which the MPU was first introduced, has a relative surface area of 9.5 compared to the surface area of the NC printed wiring boards in the Fanuc Series 16i (1997). This is larger than the relative surface area of 7.5 for the Fanuc 260, which makes full use of integrated circuits. That is to say, the introduction of the MPU, an epoch-making elemental technology, had resulted in a temporary increase in the size of the main printed circuit board in the computation unit, compared to the size prior to that introduction. This is a same upward reflection in experience curve as we observed in the reflection of Ford's shift from Model T to Model A. This suggests that the introduction of the MPU created technical issues concerning the architecture design.

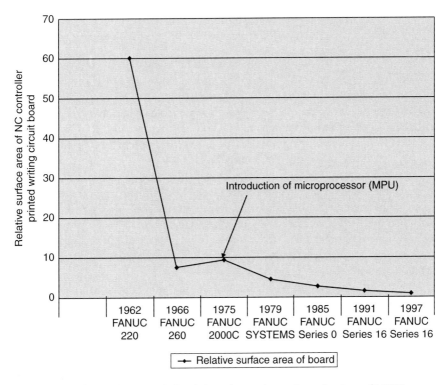

Figure 2.10 Change in printed circuit board area due to introduction of MPU

5.   Learning-by-porting

We can now go forward into the learning curve associated with architectural change. The numerically controlled (NC) machine tools have a long history. However, NC machine tools controlled by personal computers (PC) are only recently realized, because NC and PC evolved independently through their own evolutionary paths (Shibata, 2009). The two systems have reached different modular *architectural structures* through their own evolutionary paths; the PC reached "open" architecture, while the NC reached "closed" architecture. Therefore, it is difficult for these two systems to be integrated, although both are *modular* structures. Indeed, the PC-controlled NC was realized only after the NC system became an open architecture system in which three functions – *display*, calculation, and drive – were modularized and worked independently without any interferences.

Baldwin and Clark looked at the dynamic possibilities that are inherent in modular structures (Baldwin and Clark, 2000). They argue that the changes that can be imagined in a modular structure are spanned by *six* relatively simple modular operators. These operators, applied at various points and in different combinations, can generate all possible *evolutionary* paths for the structure. They define and describe the six modular operators: splitting, substituting, augmenting, excluding, inverting,[7] and porting. The "porting" operator, as the name suggests, *ports* modules to other systems and is the only operator that operates on *other* systems. The other five operators only work within their respective system. Porting occurs when a hidden module "breaks loose" and is able to *function* in more than one system.

An *embryonic* example of porting can be found in the Japanese experience of wide diffusion of the electronic boarding pass used for the mass transportation of passengers in larger cities. As everyone knows, those tasks related to the ticketing and tolling system of railroad service had been very labor-intensive. However, the tolling system is now equipped with a disruptive technology – that is, RFID (Radio Frequency Identification). This initial diffusion of the electronic boarding card system did result easily in the even wider diffusion of the electronic cashing system in the convenience stores located near the railroad stations. It was made possible by taking advantages of utilizing cash deposits, which was originally supposed to be used for balancing the deficits caused by occasional extension of trips. In short, the RFID card for mass transit tolling is "ported" into a cashing system of convenience stores. Thus, the initial introduction of RFID into mass transits evolved into a cashing system that encompasses both railroad ticket-tolling and cashing at nearby retailing stores.

In the case of the PC-controlled NC, a PC function is *ported* into the display module, as shown in Figure 2.11.

As seen in the figure, in the *second* module participation, only after the display module is *parceled out* from the whole NC system of closed architecture does the porting of PC into the NC system become possible. This porting took a much longer time than everyone had expected (Shibata, 2009). We can argue, therefore, PC-NC was realized only through a new mode of learning in *architectural*

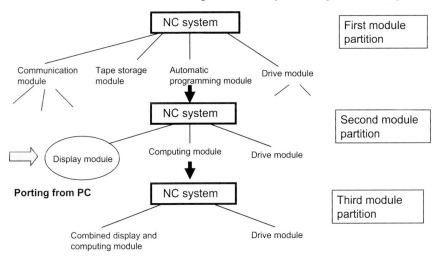

Figure 2.11 Porting a PC function in the PC-controlled NC
Source: Shibata (2009)

change – that is, "learning-by-porting" (Kodama, 2014). Good evidence of the successful adoption of "learning-by-porting" by Fanuc can be found in its long-sustained growth in terms of its total sales and profits since its establishment, as depicted in Figure 2.12. This figure also contains the performance data in terms of profit ratios which were kept consistently high throughout the company's history. This made Fanuc the most profitable company in Japan.

The integration of a PC function into the display unit of an NC, moreover, realized an NC system with flexible and enhanced PC functions such as database and networking. The database function, for example, enabled the NC operator to manage tool files, customize operation screens, and freely build human interfaces. The PC's networking function could also be used to operate the NC from a remote location within the factory via the Internet. The combination of the PC's abundant information processing functions with control functions heralded innovations that turned the NC equipment into a product with diverse uses (customer value) at a more technologically advanced level.

We can *port* a new external module to the highest-order module, while it also *diversifies* customer value. In the case of PC-NC, customer value was diversified by porting the information processing function into the product, which was not available in existing NC equipment. Furthermore, *users* can port external modules by themselves and not be dependent on vendors. For example, Mori Seiki Co., Ltd., a leading Japanese machine tool manufacturer and user of NC systems, developed their own PC-NC by *porting* consumer PCs to the display module of their NC system. Mori Seiki had been using *standard* NC equipment supplied by NC manufacturers such as Fanuc and Mitsubishi Electric. Mori Seiki *purchased* NC equipment from these manufacturers and *fitted* it onto its own machine

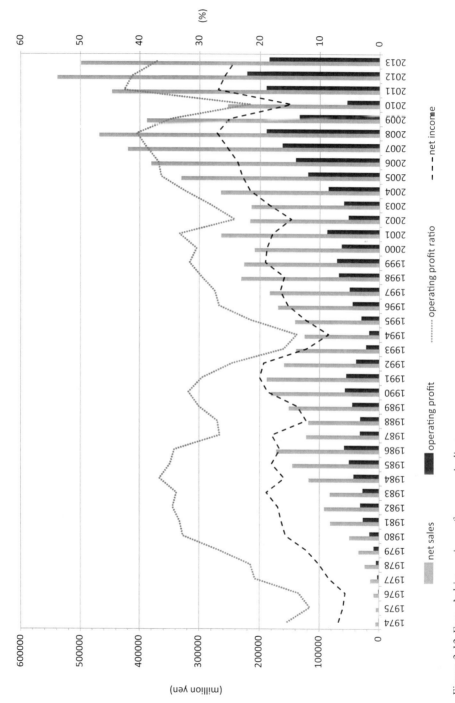

Figure 2.12 Fanuc's history in performance indicators

tools. Mori Seiki therefore developed its own operation *panel* based on PC, and designed its own PC-NC equipment by *porting* a PC-based operation panel to the display unit of the NC equipment of NC manufacturers. However, automobile manufacturers and other machine tool users were largely disadvantaged because the *usability* of operation panels differs among individual NC equipment manufacturers, complicating user operation. In other words, Mori Seiki ported PC functions developed originally for its own use to the display unit, and integrated it with the computing and driver units from NC manufacturers, creating its own PC-NC system by combining these units. Development began in 1997, and the MAPPS (Mori Advanced Programming Production System) was released in 2000. Mori Seiki has now completed the improved MAPPS III and is using it in all its models. This has *enabled* Mori Seiki to produce its own *common* specifications for operation and display methods independently of the NC equipment manufacturers.

What is the business implication of learning-by-porting? The *commoditization* of digital home electronics in recent years has been remarkable. Since industries facing commoditization have found it difficult to differentiate their products among competitors, they have been forced to engage in price competition. In this situation, companies are having difficulty generating sufficient profit despite achieving major technological innovations. The learning-by-porting offers a viable option for companies to *break away* from commoditization by diversifying and enhancing customer *value* of the product (Hsu and Lim, 2014).

By porting specific modules of modular products from other industries, learning-by-porting can expand the *value dimension* of the products, thus contributing to product differentiation. The most important customer values of NC equipment are *accuracy* and *speed*, since the role of NC equipment is to control machine tools. Thus, efforts had been made to achieve technological innovations in NC equipment in terms of high-speed and high-accuracy cutting functions. In contrast, PC-NC adapted a new *value dimension* of information-processing functions, which diversified customer value of the products. The *coexisting* values of controlling and information processing diversified the value dimension that NC provides to customers and created product concepts such as PC-NC. By diversifying the value dimension, the learning-by-porting dynamics suggests possibilities for differentiating products and breaking away from commoditization (Shibata, 2009).

6. Looking ahead

The modal shifts in technological learning, we would argue, have resulted in the global shifts in technical leadership. In the era of learning-by-doing, the global companies of the United States dominated the world economy. In the learning-by-using era, the Japanese companies emerged as one of the global technological superpowers. In the learning-by-integration era, Korean and Taiwanese companies were clearly successful in competing in the world market (Newsweek, 2005). If we look at these global phenomena carefully, we find a *coincidental* matching between the technological learning mode and the global strategy of companies in each country at each stage. We argue that global strategies of multinational American IT companies such as Google and Apple now seem to be most successfully accommodating the learning-by-porting mode.

However, there are some areas where no country has succeeded in understanding the learning mode and formulating strategies. According to Nelson (2001), it has not been well recognized that the advance of human know-how has been extremely uneven, very rapid, and cumulatively great in some fields, like communications and computation, and quite limited in other fields, like house building and education.

During the Johnson administration of the United States, a "great society" was proposed but no technological realization was accomplished.[8] In the Nixon administration, an ambitious program called RANN (Research Applied to National Needs) was at the top agenda of NSF (National Science Foundation), but disappeared when the government changed. In a similar fashion, the Japanese government proposed several programs of aggressive application of industrial technologies to social development, but were not successful in developing new types of applications.[9]

In fact, several socio-political factors turned out to be barriers for implementation, such as the financial burden involved in the Vietnam War had faded away the ideal of a "great society" program, the NSF tradition collided with RANN ideas (Green and Lepkowski, 2006), and the energy crisis in Japan gave no room for new application of technologies. An important reason for these uneven developments is, Nelson argues, that the sciences behind various technologies have advanced unevenly. We would argue, however, that several technologies more appropriate for these applications, such as RFID (Radio Frequency Identification) and GPS (Global Positioning System), are now available (Kodama, 2014). Yet, we had not succeeded in formulating appropriate strategies for implementing the goals of such programs as intended. It is because, we would argue, we have not comprehended or formulated policies which accommodate the essence of learning-by-porting.

Only through learning-by-porting can institutions and technologies co-evolve. As described above, *embryonic* evidence can be found in the Japanese experience of wide diffusion of the electronic boarding pass in mass transportation systems. As is well known, those tasks related to the ticketing and tolling system of railroad service are so labor-intensive that the system itself was designed fairly biased by strong *trade unionism* of railroad business to avoid manpower layoffs, as is common in every country. However, the tolling system is now equipped with the disruptive technology (i.e., RFID) since this radical technology makes it possible to mechanize almost all the tasks related to ticketing and tolling, without any *protest* from any trade union. This is because RFID technology was so smoothly ported to the ticketing and tolling practices that no one was able to notice or claim that the new system created a kind of *dehumanization*.

We also described above that the initial diffusion of the electronic boarding card system resulted easily in the even wider diffusion of the electronic cashing system in convenience stores located near the railroad stations. In terms of porting, this case can be interpreted as the two stages of "porting." The first is that the RFID card is "ported" into the ticketing and tolling system of mass transits. The second is that this RFID card is "ported" into the cashing system of convenience stores. Thus, the initial introduction of RFID into mass transits evolved into cashing systems at nearby retailing stores. Based on this experience, we can argue, they can further expand the technology applications into different sectors of society one after another by means of multi-stage porting. In conclusion, a multiple implementation of learning-by-porting may make it possible for both technology and institutions to co-evolve with each other simultaneously and smoothly.

Notes

1 A mismatch might have existed between the mode of learning and the system of learning, which was very often determined by political ideology. In his book called *The End of History*, Francis Fukuyama (1992) put forth a question: why Marx Leninism failed in making a smooth transition into a post-industrial society. His response to this question is this: the Soviet system was built around the early industrialization in the steel and shipbuilding industries as they were developed. However, the industrial society moved into the industrial system in which the role of information technology has overridden that of heavy industry. While other industrialized countries made this transition more or less smoothly, the gap between the technological and the political systems had remained inept in the USSR.

2 This ideal of steel-making had become a reality when a German, S. Junghans, invented the mold vibration mechanism for copper and aluminum in 1934. This success paved the way toward continuous casting of steel-making. In the 1940s, the advanced countries including the USSR made concerted efforts for producing steel by means of continuous casting.

3 These heavy machinery suppliers include the following companies: IH1 Heavy Industries, Shimazu Machinery, Toshiba Co., Hitachi Co., Yasukawa Electric, Kawasaki Heavy Industries, Sumitomo Machinery, Sumitomo Electric Industries, Hitachi Shipbuilding, Fujitsu, Fuji Electric Co., Mitsubishi Heavy Industries, and Mitsubishi Electric Co.

4 According to the statistics (1982–1998) compiled by the Korean Ministry of Education, as many as 16,255 PhDs were obtained by Koreans in foreign countries, about half of which are in either science or engineering – 4,602 in engineering and 3,188 in natural sciences. The majority of them are US PhD holders – 9,904 from US universities, 2,490 from Japan, 1,369 from West Germany, 835 from France, and 427 from the UK. To sum up, this large number of Korean technical talents was more than enough to accommodate the learning-by-integration process.

5 The conventional paradigm is that the development of a generic technology automatically brings diversification by applying the technology to various kinds of products. In this view, a technology is developed first for a technologically demanding, high-end product, and then extended for the use of less technologically demanding, low-end products through the development of low-cost, quality-controlled mass-production processes. According to this view, diversification is based on the "spin-off" principle.

6 NC systems have various functions such as motor driving functions, in addition to the arithmetic and logic operations that are provided by the MPU. Therefore, a coordinated execution of those functions for the systems as a whole is made only possible by *integration* of those functions.

7 According to Baldwin and Clark, designers achieve modularity by partitioning information into *visible* design rules and *hidden* design parameters (Baldwin and Clark, 2000). The operator "inversion" describes the action of taking previously hidden information and "moving it up" the design hierarchy so that it is visible to a group of modules.

8 Sources are: http://www.ushistory.org/us/56e.asp; http://countrystudies.us/united-states/history-121.htm; http://www.colorado.edu/AmStudies/lewis/2010/gresoc.htm; https://www.boundless.com/u-s-history/the-sixties-1960–1969/the-lyndon-b-johnson-administration/the-great-society/.

9 Japan had similar experiences during the 1970s and 1990s. The first of those experiences occurred just before the first world oil crisis. The Economic Planning Agency organized a science and technology committee for planning of "societal development." The question asked was why science and technology, which were so effective for Japanese economic development, cannot be mobilized for building social capital. They said that it was time for Japan to pay more attention to the quality of life. This interest disappeared so easily because of the panic brought by the oil embargo.

   The second experience was the establishment of MITI's committee on societal systems, which discussed the applications of industrial high technologies to the efficient building of social infrastructures. The rationale behind these ideas was that the frontiers for technology development was shifting from industry to social capital development, and that technical innovations also shifted from sector-specific technologies to various system technologies across several industrial sectors. Several social experiments had been conducted at the foot of Mount Fuji by the Japan Association for Promoting Machinery Industries. But nothing came out from these experiments.

   In May of 1997, Hashimoto's Prime Minister Office published the action plan for restructuring the Japanese industrial structure. The key wording was "creation of new industries." They specified fifteen sectors for new industries such as "Information and Communications Industry" and "Industry for Developing City and its Environments." In both of these two sectors, the Intelligent Transport System (ITS) was cited an example of a new industry. In the Information and Communication sector, the ITS is the new product and service generated by combining Information/Communication Technology with Mechanical technologies. In the City-related sector, it is the creation of a "new transportation system" with the use of the most advanced ICTs. But they were all premature technologically – that is, no appropriate technologies were available.

Reference

Abernathy, W., and Wayne, K. (1974), "Limits of the learning curve", *Harvard Business Review*, September-October 1974, pp. 109–118.

Arrow, K. (1962), "The economic implication of learning by doing", *Review of Economic Studies*, vol. 29, no. 3, pp. 155–173.

Baldwin, C., and Clark, K. (2000), *Design Rules: The Power of Modularity*, Cambridge: MIT Press.

Bateson, G. (1973), *Steps to an Ecology of Mind*, London: Paladin.

Branscomb, L. (1989), "Policy for science and engineering in 1989: A public agenda for economic renewal", *Business in the Contemporary World*, vol. 2, no. 1, pp. 69–80.

Fukuyama, F. (1992), *The End of History and the Last Man*, Perennial: Imprint of Harper Collins Publishers.

Green, R., and Lepkowski, W. (2006), "A forgotten model for purposeful science", *Issues in Science and Technology*, Winter issue, vol. 22, no. 2, pp. 69–73.

Henderson, R., and Clark, K. (1990), "Architectural innovation: The re-configuration of existing product technologies and the failure of established firms", *Administrative Science Quarterly*, March issue, vol. 35, no. 1, pp. 9–30.

Hsu, D., and Lim, K. (2014), "Knowledge brokering and organizational innovation: Founder imprinting effects", *Organizational Science*, vol. 25, no. 4, pp. 1134–1153.

Japan Steel Association (1996), *Japanese History of Continuous Casting for Steel Making*, Tokyo.

Kim, L. (1997), *Imitation to Innovation*, Boston: Harvard Business School Press, pp. 40–41.

Kodama, F. (1995), *Emerging Patterns of Innovation*, Boston: Harvard Business School Press.

Kodama, F. (1999), "The Japanese pattern: Knowledge creation through learning-by-using in the Japanese industry", presented at the conference *Promise of Science as Opportunity for Development*, Madrid.

Kodama, F. (2014), "MOT in transition: From technology fusion to technology-service convergence", *Technovation*, vol. 34, no. 9, pp. 505–512.

Kodama F., et al. (1998), *Core Competencies of the Japanese Steel Industry*, Japan Steel Association, pp. 6–43, Toyko.

Nakata, Y. (2005), "Why is Asia Pacific so strong in liquid crystal display industry? Approach from industrial architectures of liquid crystal display", Proceedings of PICMET'05 (Portland International Conference on Management of Engineering and Technology), August 2005, USA.

Nakata, Y. (2009), "Product design and interdependencies analyzed by design structure matrix: Comparative research of liquid crystal display and semiconductor", *Design Principles & Practices: An International Journal*, vol. 3, no. 2, pp. 1–16.

Nelson, R, and Sampat, B. (2001), "Making sense of institutions as a factor shaping economic performance", *Journal of Economic Behavior and Organization*, vol. 44, no. 1, pp. 31–54.

Newsweek (2005), *News Asian Business*, May 16, pp. 18–24.

Nikkei Micro-Devices Supervision (2007), Production Line of TFT-LCD, Flat Panel Display 2008 (Markets New Application Edition).

Nonaka, L. (1990), *A Theory of Organizational Knowledge Creation* (in Japanese), Nippon Keizai Shimbun Co., Tokyo.

Noyce, R. (1979), "Microelectronics", *Science* (in Japanese), September, Tokyo.

Porter, M. (1979), "How competitive forces shape strategy", *Harvard Business Review*, March-April, pp. 137–145.

Rosenberg, N. (1982), *Inside the Black Box: Technology and Economics*, Cambridge: Cambridge University Press.

Sato, S. (1996), "Technology transfer in modern times" (in Japanese), *Technology Development* (Kaihatsu-Gijyutsu), vol.1, no. 2, p. 67.

Shibata, T. (2009), "Product innovation through module dynamics", *Journal of Engineering and Technology Management*, vol. 26, no. 1–2, pp. 46–56.

Shibata, T., Yano, M., and Kodama, F. (2005), "Empirical analysis of evolution of product architecture Fanuc numerical controllers from 1962 to 1997", *Research Policy*, vol. 34, no. 1, pp. 13–31.

Tomiura, A. (1997), "Productivity in Japan's manufacturing industry", *International Journal of Production Economics*, vol. 52, no. 1–2, pp. 239–246.

3 Innovations and networks

George A. Barnett

1. Introduction

This chapter discusses the innovation process and how innovations, new products, practices, or ideas are created and then diffused from a network analytic perspective. It begins by describing the network paradigm. Next, it describes a series of examples of the application of the network perspective to the innovation process at the cognitive, individual, and organizational levels. Then, it makes a number of actionable recommendations that managers can take to facilitate individual and organizational innovation by taking advantage of knowledge about information and social networks. The chapter ends by describing the diffusion of innovations and the role of social networks in this process.

Network analysis is a set of research procedures for identifying *structures* in systems based on the patterns of *relations* among system components, where the components – typically called nodes, vertices, actors, or agents – may be words or concepts, individuals, teams or work groups, information sources such as the mass media or the world-wide web, organizations, or nation-states, and the system may be an individual's cognitions, small task groups, organizations, communities, nations, the Internet, or even the entire world as a whole. Typically, the relations are called links, ties, or edges. In communication science, the ties are the frequency of information transfer in its many forms among these components, although in the other social sciences the relations among the components may be based on power, advice, conflict, friendship, cognitive stimuli such as words, the actors' joint activities or shared affiliations, as well as diseases, material, or work flows.

The goal of network analysis is to describe the structure of the higher-level system based on the pattern of linkages among the set of lower-level nodes and, hopefully, how this structure changes over time in response to events both internal and external to the system that may be natural or human-made. For example, network analysis can describe the structure of an organization based on the communication relations among its members and how the organizational structure changes as a result of a new technology. It differs from traditional social research by focusing on the *relationships* among the components rather than the attributes of individual nodes. As a result, network analysis provides new insights into individual behavior and social processes that were not revealed by the analysis of individuals. Hopefully, this chapter will bring to light insights into the process by which new products, practices, or ideas are conceived and diffused, which may be applied by individuals and organizations to facilitate their creation.

2. Cognitive networks

Let me begin at the individual level, specifically at the cognitive level, by asking, where do new ideas come from? Simply, new ideas are formed from old ones. Complex ideas are composed of a set of associations or relations among simple atomistic elements or concepts. The arrangement or structure of these elements that forms cognition is contingent on the information that individuals have previously received. Since we generally consider concepts or words to be the basic unit of cognition and the relationship among the words to express meaning, cognitive networks are often called semantic networks. There are many ways to describe this network, including neural networks, spatial models, and graph theoretical models.

Neural networks suggest that the structure of cognition at any point in time is given by the state of the network underlying that cognition and that cognitive processes are defined by the changing patterns of activation of the nodes in a network (Woelfel, 1993). The state of any node is a function of the energy flows that define it. At the simplest level, a node may be turned on or off. This set of nodes will define a network, and the resulting pattern of their activation indicates the network's structure. For example, consider the neural network presented in Figure 3.1 composed of a series of automobiles, the attributes used to describe

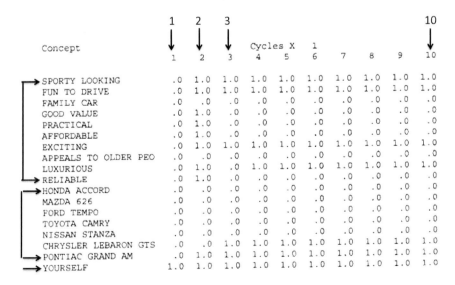

Concept	1	2	3	4	5	6	7	8	9	10
SPORTY LOOKING	.0	1.0	1.0	1.0	1.0	1.0	1.0	1.0	1.0	1.0
FUN TO DRIVE	.0	1.0	1.0	1.0	1.0	1.0	1.0	1.0	1.0	1.0
FAMILY CAR	.0	.0	.0	.0	.0	.0	.0	.0	.0	.0
GOOD VALUE	.0	1.0	.0	.0	.0	.0	.0	.0	.0	.0
PRACTICAL	.0	1.0	.0	.0	.0	.0	.0	.0	.0	.0
AFFORDABLE	.0	1.0	.0	.0	.0	.0	.0	.0	.0	.0
EXCITING	.0	1.0	1.0	1.0	1.0	1.0	1.0	1.0	1.0	1.0
APPEALS TO OLDER PEO	.0	.0	.0	.0	.0	.0	.0	.0	.0	.0
LUXURIOUS	.0	1.0	.0	1.0	1.0	1.0	1.0	1.0	1.0	1.0
RELIABLE	.0	1.0	.0	.0	.0	.0	.0	.0	.0	.0
HONDA ACCORD	.0	.0	.0	.0	.0	.0	.0	.0	.0	.0
MAZDA 626	.0	.0	.0	.0	.0	.0	.0	.0	.0	.0
FORD TEMPO	.0	.0	.0	.0	.0	.0	.0	.0	.0	.0
TOYOTA CAMRY	.0	.0	.0	.0	.0	.0	.0	.0	.0	.0
NISSAN STANZA	.0	.0	.0	.0	.0	.0	.0	.0	.0	.0
CHRYSLER LEBARON GTS	.0	.0	1.0	1.0	1.0	1.0	1.0	1.0	1.0	1.0
PONTIAC GRAND AM	.0	1.0	1.0	1.0	1.0	1.0	1.0	1.0	1.0	1.0
YOURSELF	1.0	1.0	1.0	1.0	1.0	1.0	1.0	1.0	1.0	1.0

Figure 3.1 Automobile neural network

Note: This figure was taken from Woefel (1993).

them and one's self concept, at a series of points in time. At time 1, the self is activated. Due to its associations with the other concepts, it turns on the concept *Pontiac*, and the attributes *sporty, fun to drive, good value, practical, affordable, exciting, luxurious,* and *reliable* at time 2. Which in turn activates *Chrysler*, and turns off *good value, practical, affordable, luxurious,* and *reliable* at time 3. After ten iterations the self is associated with *sporty, fun to drive, exciting, luxurious,* and the two automobiles. Assuming that this example is based on empirical data, this neural network may be used to describe a consumer's cognitive network regarding automobiles and models designed that is consistent with their cognitive network.

Cognitive networks may also be displayed using spatial models. Figure 3.2 shows a spatial model of a series of soft drinks and their attributes. The distance between any pair of nodes indicates their strength of association, such that the closer two nodes are, the stronger their association. Notice that all the cola terms are located in the bottom left quadrant and the lemon-lime drinks in the upper right. This diagram was used to develop "Pepsi Pure", a clear Pepsi, in an attempt to reposition a cola drink closer to the ideal beverage.

The third model of cognition is the traditional graph theoretic link-node model. Figure 3.3 shows the semantic network concerning tobacco control. At the center of the network is the concept *tobacco*. It has direct ties to *health, prevention,* and *eliminate,* as well as a number of other concepts. The thicker the line between two words, the stronger the tie between them.

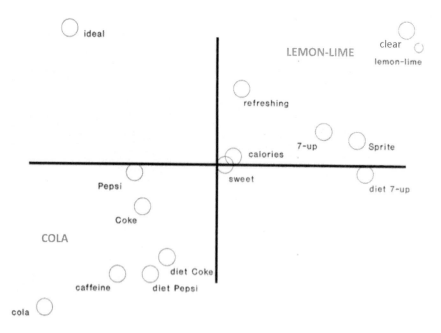

Figure 3.2 Spatial model of soft drinks

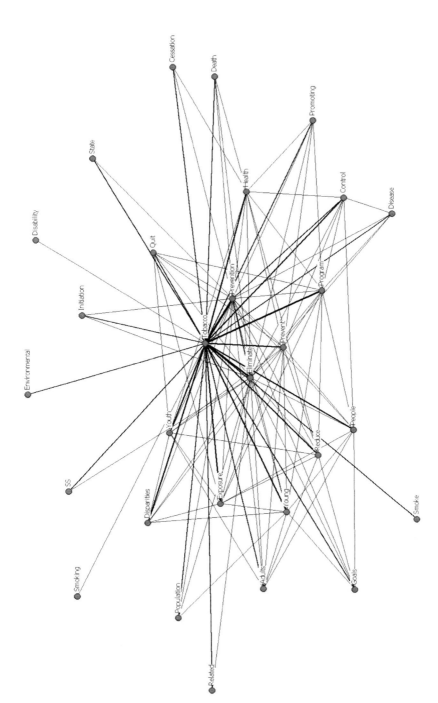

Figure 3.3 Graph theoretical model of tobacco control

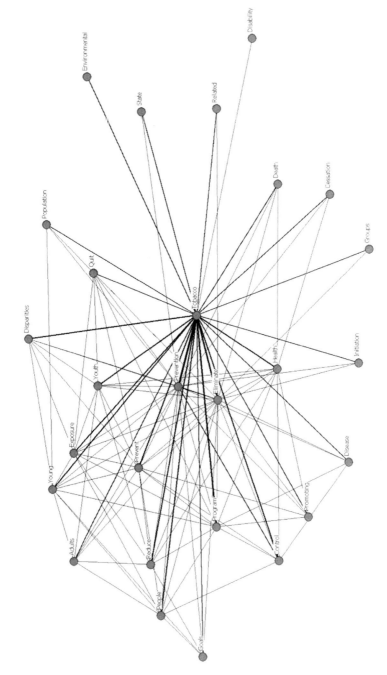

Figure 3.4 Graph theoretical model of tobacco control with the concept smoke removed

Innovation occurs when the elements are rearranged in a manner that they haven't been before. This occurs in three ways:

1   A new concept enters the same cognitive domain (network) of the innovator as the existing concepts. For example, consider smokeless tobacco, such as the e-cigarette. How might the current network be reorganized as a result of the addition of this concept?
2   A concept may be removed from this domain, which previously prevented the individual from relating them in a novel manner. In the example shown in Figure 3.4, smoke, smoking, and secondhand smoke were removed from the same cognitive domain and produced the following cognitive network.
3   The elements may be rearranged so that they may be observed from a different perspective. For example, in Figure 3.5, *Pepsi* is relocated in the network by weakening its tie with *caffeine* and strengthening its tie to *clear*.

3.   Individual social/information networks

Since the arrangement of cognitive elements is contingent upon an individual's prior information, a necessary condition for innovation is for individuals to have new experiences. Innovation is a function of the variety and scope of information sources to which the individual is exposed. Therefore, to stimulate innovation, you want to expose people to a wide variety of information sources, both within

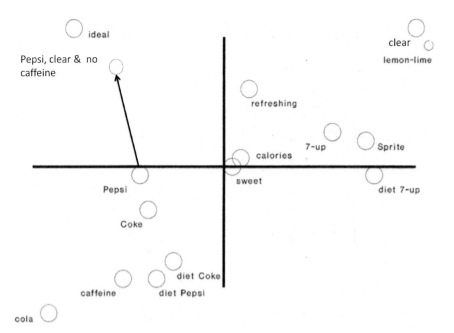

Figure 3.5 Spatial model of soft drinks with concepts rearranged

their own area of technical expertise and from other areas that only require a lay understanding.

Research done some time ago by my students had scientists and engineers categorize their peers as innovative, productive, or neither innovative nor productive. Then, the students examined the scientists' and engineers' media use patterns and their interpersonal networks. They found that the innovative scientists and engineers read both within their field of expertise and also popular and general interest materials. They had friends from a wide variety of backgrounds, traveled widely, and had other interests besides their research. The productive scholars tended to read only within their area of expertise and had inter-locking social networks composed of individuals like themselves. The non-innovative, non-productive individuals tended not to read and tended to be social isolates. The information networks for these three types of individuals are displayed in Figure 3.6. In this case, the nodes are information sources. They may be individuals, reading materials, or other sources of information.

Note that the innovative scientist has what is known as a radial social network. The individuals do not communicate with each other. The productive scientist, however, has an integrated or interlocking network. Everyone communicates with each other. The non-innovative or non-productive person is an isolate. He/she has no communicative ties to anyone. Each tie in a radial network exposes

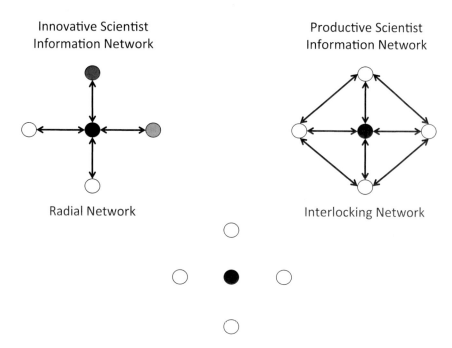

Figure 3.6 Three types of individuals' information networks

an individual to unique information, while all the ties in an interlocking network provide the same information. After the individual learns the information from the first contact, all future interactions are redundant, simply repeating old ideas and the social norms of the interconnected group. The isolated individual receives no information.

4. Stimulating individual innovation

How does one stimulate innovation? You want to make available a wide variety of information.

Mediated communication: (1) journals (technical and trades), (2) popular, business, or general interest magazines, (3) newspapers (hard copy and online), (4) video, (5) high-speed Internet access without restriction about how people use it.

Interpersonal communication: put people in situations where they come into contact with new people and ideas. (1) Send them to conferences, workshops, and seminars, not just about their area of expertise but where they would be exposed to novel ideas. (2) Academic experiences (pay for an advanced education and allow sabbaticals to go to school). (3) Outside speakers (not just with technical expertise but speakers to stimulate thought). (4) Join inter-organizational groups, such as trade groups, where people can share ideas with others with whom they wouldn't ordinarily come into contact.

To stimulate innovation, you want people to establish network ties to those individuals and organizations that may provide new and different perspectives. Such opportunities occur at clubs (local chapter of ACM, golf, or tennis clubs), at sports and cultural events, or at community organizations (church, civic organizations). One wants many connections, lots of boundary-spanning links, ties to individuals from different social systems. However, at the same time you want to keep integration low. You don't want people networking with others from the same position in the social system. This only makes the ties redundant, and people will only hear old ideas, which takes time and energy away from new ideas.

Direct experience: give people novel direct experiences such as through international travel. Allow the freedom to experiment and the time to try out new ideas. Google allows its employees at least 10 percent of their work time to experiment with their own ideas. This section discussed how to stimulate individual innovation through interpersonal communication and direct experience.

5. Stimulating organizational innovation

All this is fine for getting individuals thinking, stimulating new ideas, but what about organizations? Organizations must be designed to build networks where people share their ideas with other members from different parts of the organization.

This may be done by the following:

1   Create many lateral links to others at equivalent levels in the organization, but located in functionally different departments or remote locations.

2   Use information and communication technologies such as web-seminars and teleconferences to exchange ideas, especially where the members are not physically co-present.
3   Encourage boundary spanning with suppliers, customers, universities, and any other individual or organization that will provide the opportunities to bring new ideas into the organization.
4   Remember to create connections but not too-integrated networks. Don't send everyone to the same events. Encourage diversity of experience.
5   Create diverse teams, such as what Steve Jobs did with the Apple Mac, where the design team included computer scientists, engineers, artists, marketing people, programmers, and designers.
6   Organizations must create time and activities, both formal and informal, that facilitate the sharing of these new thoughts in a positive organizational culture, like brown-bag lunches and in-house seminars.

But the question remains, how do you get people to read these publications, use information-orientated media, and participate in these educational experiences and experiment? This is done by creating an organizational culture that rewards the reading and discussion of new ideas so that one doesn't put down different ideas and that rewards those who champion new ideas.

From a human resources perspective, hire people with diverse backgrounds. Create a database of their backgrounds. What courses did they take at the university? What were their majors? What projects have they worked on in the past? What are their hobbies and other personal interests? Where have they traveled? What are their research interests? Then use this database to help form diverse teams composed of individuals with special expertise relevant to the specific projects. This section of the chapter suggested ways to stimulate innovation at the organizational level.

6.   Network models of diffusion

The information network of an individual may be placed in context by describing the patterns of communication for an entire social system to describe the process by which innovations diffuse. Figure 3.7 shows the ego-centric or personal network for the white node. Those dark nodes that are connected to it are its sources of information, information about new products, practices, and ideas. As early as the mid-1950s, Coleman, Katz, and Menzel (1966) reported that a person's social connection to his or her local colleagues was strongly related to time of adoption. Individuals seemed to learn from one another, while those only weakly connected to others tended to learn from outside sources such as change agents and the mass media. Sociometric ties to colleagues who adopted the innovation appeared to reduce the uncertainty or risk involved with its adoption.

Let's consider the white node. What proportion of his/her first-order links (direct contacts) must adopt before he/she adopts? In other words, what is

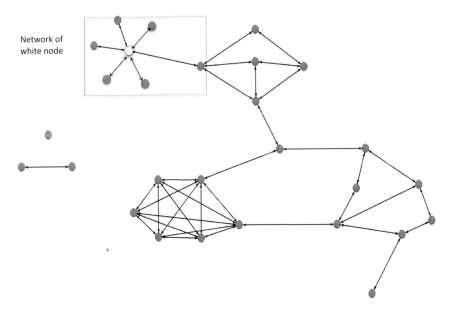

Network of
white node

Figure 3.7 An individual information network embedded in an entire social system

his/her adoption threshold? According to social influence theory, if we assume that all contacts are equivalent (a homogenous social network) in terms of the frequency of interaction, the ability to persuade, and credibility, then it should be 50 percent plus. That is, if the majority of the white node's contacts adopt (4 of 6), then he/she will adopt. Of course, we can always weight these contacts by the strength of the tie with the focal node (frequency of interaction, perceived credibility: expertise, trustworthiness, or medium of communication used to provide information about the innovation). Further, this notion does not take into account the attributes of the innovation, its cost, relative advantage (economic and social), compatibility, complexity, trialability, and observability (Rogers, 2003). Also, assume that the innovation does not violate system norms regarding adopting something new. But, of course, innovations do vary in these attributes, and individuals vary in willingness to take risks. For innovations without much cost or risk associated with their adoption, one's threshold will be less than 50 percent, and, for those expensive innovations that entail a great deal of risk, more than the majority might be required. Further, certain individuals are what Everett Rogers (2003) labeled early adopters. They are risk takers and have lower adoption thresholds than those individuals he labeled as early or late majority.

But the threshold model represents only a small part of the network model of diffusion. Do earlier adopters simply have lower thresholds, or are their social networks different, with links outside their immediate social group? They tend to have links outside the social system. They are boundary spanners. In Rogers' terminology, they are cosmopolite. As indicated earlier, innovators tend to have patterns of linkage of this type. Note the highlighted node in Figure 3.8.

And what about those individuals who are late adopters, often called laggards? They tend to be only weakly connected to others in the network, the dark gray node at the bottom of Figure 3.8. What about those who never adopt an innovation? Generally, they are social isolates, the black node in the figure. Thus, a node's position in a social network determines his/her time of adoption.

The structure of the network also determines the rate of an innovation's adoption, again controlling for the attributes of the innovation. The rate of adoption is faster for centralized networks, provided that the nodes at core adopt. These individuals tend to be opinion leaders. Denser networks, those with more links, tend to adopt innovations more quickly than sparse networks. And networks with more weak ties adopt more quickly (Granovetter, 1982). These bridge links and ties involving liaisons speed up the diffusion process by connecting the subgroups in a social network. This is shown in Figure 3.9.

Also, the rate of adoption depends on where the innovation is first adopted in the social system. Rogers (2003) writes that the first adopters, the innovators, tend to be somewhat peripheral due to their idiosyncratic interest in the "new" product, practice, or idea. After the initial adopters demonstrate the feasibility of the innovation, it is then taken up by early adopters, who tend to be high-status opinion leaders. They have the resources necessary to minimize the risk of adoption, resulting in lower adoption thresholds. They tend to be at the center of the social network. The early adopters influence the other nodes (the early majority) to adopt the innovation. Eventually, all the connected nodes will adopt. This process is represented in Figure 3.10.

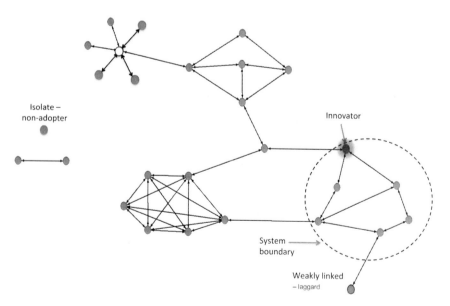

Figure 3.8 Networks and diffusion with system boundaries and roles

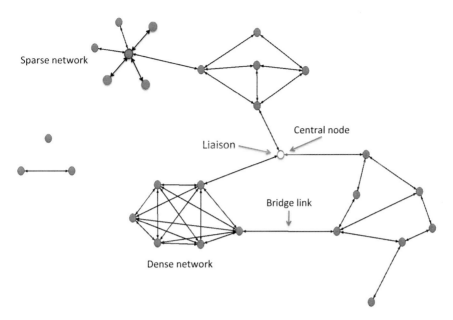

Sparse network

Central node

Liaison

Bridge link

Dense network

Figure 3.9 Networks and diffusion-network roles and the rate of adoption

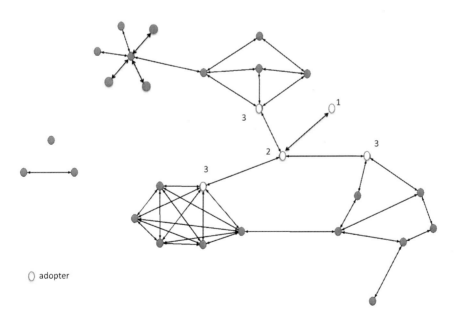

adopter

Figure 3.10 Networks and the diffusion process

Notes: The white nodes are adopters. The numbers indicate their time of adoption, with 1 being the first to adopt.

The network model of diffusion is not without its limitations. It assumes an internal influence model. That is, information is spread internally within a social system only through interpersonal ties. It does not take into account external influences that come from mediated sources, although the external source may initiate the diffusion process. Recent research by Jim Danowski, Gluesing, and Riopelle (2011) suggests that innovations spread within organizations through the digital media, such as email, are adopted in much the same way as from an external source. Thus, the network model of diffusion presented here may not directly apply for diffusion through Facebook and Twitter and other social media.

Also, the network model does not take reinvention; modifications in the innovation to accommodate individual needs, tastes, or personal situations; or dis-adoption due to dissatisfaction with the innovation or substitution by a newer innovation that better meets the individual's needs or desires into account (Nam and Barnett, 2010). Recently, however, state-of-the-art simulations have tested models of diffusion with competing innovations (Tutzauer, Kwon, and Elbirt, 2011).

7.   Concluding remarks

This chapter discussed the innovation process and how innovations, new products, practices, or ideas are created and then diffused from a network analytic perspective. It began by describing the network paradigm. Next, it described a series of examples that applied the network perspective to the innovation process at the cognitive, individual, and organizational levels. Importantly, it made a number of actionable recommendations that managers can take to facilitate individual and organizational innovation by using knowledge about information and social networks in their company. The chapter concluded by describing the diffusion of innovations and the role of social networks in this process.

Many scholars from around the world are continuing to conduct research using network models to examine the process of innovation and their diffusion throughout organizations, individual societies, and the world as a whole. For example, Arun Vishwanath has conducted extensive research on the cognitive networks of consumers to predict their acceptance of new communication technologies and has examined the impact of cultural differences on the perceptions of these products (Vishwanath, 2009; Vishwanath and Chen, 2006; Vishwanath and Barnett, 2011).

Another social scientist, Thomas Valente (1994), has written extensively and continues to conduct research on the role of social networks in the diffusion process. His work on thresholds for adoption (Valente, 1996) and opinion leadership in the diffusion process (Iyengar, Van den Bulte, and Valente, 2011) have been seminal in our understanding of social networks in the diffusion process. Worth noting is his research on accelerating the diffusion of innovations through the application of knowledge learned by examining community social networks (Valente, 2012).

My own research develops mathematical models to examine the process of the adoption and disadoption of technological innovations (Barnett, 2011), and the impact of perturbations such as the development and diffusion of new technologies on the structure of social networks (Barnett, 2014; Barnett, Ruiz, Hammond, and Xin, 2013). The research on cognitive and social networks and their role in the innovation process continues. I sense that future advances in our understanding of these processes will have a profound impact on how we view innovation and our ability to facilitate the creation and spread of new technologies in the future. I encourage you to think about network ties at both the cognitive and the social levels when attempting to facilitate the innovation process and to focus your attention on developments in this field of inquiry.

References

Barnett, G. A. (2011), "Mathematical models of the diffusion process", in Vishwanath, A., and Barnett, G. A. (eds.), *The Diffusion of Innovations: A Communication Science Perspective*, pp. 103–122, New York: Peter Lang.

Barnett, G. A. (2014), Using Coherencies to Examine Network Evolution, Paper presented to the International Communication Association, Seattle.

Barnett, G. A., Ruiz, J. B., Hammond, J. R., and Xin, Z. (2013), "An examination of the relationship between international telecommunication networks, terrorism and global news coverage", *Social Networks and Mining*, vol. 3, no. 3, pp. 721–747. (DOI) 10.1007/s13278–013–0117–9.

Coleman, J. S., Katz, E., and Menzel, H. (1966), *Medical Innovations: A Diffusion Study*, New York: Bobbs-Merrill.

Danowski, J. A., Gluesing, J., and Riopelle, K. (2011), "The revolution in diffusion theory caused by new media", in Vishwanath, A., and Barnett, G. A. (eds.), *The Diffusion of Innovations: A Communication Science Perspective*, pp. 123–144, New York: Peter Lang.

Granovetter, M. S. (1982), "The strength of weak ties: A network theory revisited", in Marsden (ed.), *Social Structure and Network Analysis*, pp. 105–130, Newbury Park, CA: Sage.

Iyengar, R., Van den Bulte, C., and Valente, T. W. (2011), "Opinion leadership and social cognition in new product diffusion", *Marketing Science*, vol. 30, no. 2, pp. 195–212.

Nam, Y., and Barnett, G. A. (2010), "Communication media diffusion and substitution: Longitudinal trends from 1980 to 2005 in Korea", *New Media & Society*, vol. 12, no. 4, pp. 1–19.

Rogers, E. M. (2003), *Diffusion of Innovation* (5th edition), New York: Free Press.

Tutzauer, F., Kwon, K., and Elbirt, B. (2011), "Network diffusion of two competing ideas", in Vishwanath, A., and Barnett, G. A. (eds.), *The Diffusion of Innovations: A Communication Science Perspective*, pp. 145–170, New York: Peter Lang.

Valente, T. W. (1994), *Network Models of the Diffusion of Innovation*, Cresskill, NJ: Hampton Press.

Valente, T. W. (1996), "Social network thresholds in the diffusion of innovations", *Social Networks*, vol. 18, no. 1, pp. 69–89.

Valente, T. W. (2012), "Network interventions", *Science*, vol. 337, no. 6090, pp. 49–53.

Vishwanath, A. (2009), "From belief-importance to intention: The impact of framing on technology adoption", *Communication Monographs*, vol. 76, no. 2, pp. 177–206.

Vishwanath, A., and Barnett, G. A. (2011), *The Diffusion of Innovations: A Communication Science Perspective*, New York: Peter Lang.

Vishwanath, A., and Chen, H. (2006), "Technology clusters: Using multidimensional scaling to evaluate and structure technology clusters", *Journal of the American Society for Information Science and Technology*, vol. 57, no. 11, pp. 1451–1460.

Woelfel, J. (1993), *Galileo Oresme: Users Manual*, Amherst, NY: The Galileo Company.

Part II

How to navigate convergence innovation

4 Convergence innovation in the management of large firms

Samsung Electronics

Jong-Yong Yun and Changsu Kim

1. Introduction

The great historian Dr. Arnold Joseph Toynbee described human history with the law of challenge and response in his masterpiece, *A Study of History*. He highlighted the notion that humanity's response to change has been the driving force for the advancement of civilization and history in human society. The law of challenge and response has been constant throughout world history, which shows that individuals and organizations that were satisfied with the existing ways and did not respond adequately to new changes had to hand over their places to those that accommodated new innovations quickly. We are now standing at a turning point in our society, moving toward the intellectualization of individuals, the digitization of society, and the globalization of nations. In particular, new revolutions brought about by the convergence innovation of information and communication technology present new challenges to every individual, enterprise, and nation (Bradley, Madnick, and Kim, 2015).

Convergence innovation is the paradigm whereby digital technologies, creativity, design, and knowledge of liberal arts are merged together and applied to areas of product, process, personnel, and information infrastructure in order to create more efficient and competitive organizations. Convergence innovation is regarded as a vital enabler for growth not only for enterprises but also for nations. The competitiveness of enterprises and nations tends to be impacted by how quickly they adapt to new trends such as convergence innovation (Abene and Newton, 2005). This chapter aims to provide insight on convergence innovation by reviewing the ways in which Samsung Electronics actively responded to changes brought about by the digital revolution.

Samsung Electronics Co., Ltd., is a multinational electronics company headquartered in Suwon, South Korea. In terms of revenue, it has been the world's largest information technology company since 2009. In recent years, it has become the world's largest manufacturer of mobile phones and smartphones, a phenomenon fueled by the popularity of its Samsung Galaxy devices. Samsung Electronics has been able to transform into a global digital company because it coped well with the paradigm shift, especially with respect to the digital revolution and convergence innovation (Yun, 2003). The process of advancing convergence innovation in the organization required the firm to surmount various difficulties, which it was ultimately able to do, allowing it to become one of the world's top enterprises. The main aim of this chapter is to take a look at the convergence innovation executed by Samsung Electronics, as well as the ways in which the company was able to overcome the challenges it faced.

The remainder of the chapter proceeds as follows: the next section describes management and convergence innovation. Section 3 presents a brief discussion of advancement in human history and the recognition of a digital revolution. Section 4 addresses the convergence innovation executed by Samsung Electronics, followed by lessons learned from that innovation. The final section summarizes the core implications.

2.   Management and convergence innovation

2.1   What is management?

Management involves efficient allocation of resources, careful planning of processes, and working toward successful innovation activities in order to achieve given business objectives. Therefore, any discussion of a firm's management first requires an examination of its direction and objectives. The main objectives of a firm tend to involve the pursuit of profitability, stability (a sound financial structure), sustainable growth, and contributions to society. Firms form organizations which run their businesses by investing capital in order to achieve these objectives.

Management entails the creation of products and services, as well as the processes by which profits are generated by selling those products and services. Management is composed of supply chain and decision-making processes, and the configuration of resources such as labor, technologies, information, and time (speed). In order for management to be effective, high-quality resources should be used to enable speedy and optimized processes for producing superb products and services that meet customers' expectations and maximize overall profits. In addition, firms should make sustained efforts to innovate, so that their resources and processes can survive in a competitive market. Corporate management has been changing and developing under the influence of business environments.

Core components of management – including resources, processes, products, and services – have evolved like those of living creatures in accordance with the changes in the business environments, including innovation based on science and technology, growth of industries, and advances in information and communication technology (ICT). In this regard, management resources and processes should be continuously innovated in order to ensure firms' survival and growth in constantly changing business environments (Abene and Newton, 2005). Therefore, management can be defined as carefully planned use of resources and processes that also involves a series of successive innovation activities.

2.2   What is convergence innovation?

Core components of management include products, processes, personnel, information infrastructure systems, and management resources, which are also targets of convergence innovation. Here, "products" refer to the objects being managed and produced by the company. "Processes" include the supply chain process, which entails developing, producing, manufacturing, and selling products and services. Other processes include the provision of after-sales services, as well as managing personnel, accounting matters, and decision-making processes. "Personnel" refers to people and organizations that manage and operate resources and processes (Chang, 2012). "Information infrastructure systems" connect people, organizations, and processes both horizontally and vertically in order to support decision-making tasks. Information infrastructure systems also include management information systems such as ERP (Enterprise Resource Planning), which handles and manages overall management data (Abene and Newton, 2005). Management "resources" include labor, technologies, capital, and time (speed).

Convergence innovation in management is a business activity, the goal of which is to build more efficient and competitive organizations by merging digital technologies, creativity, design, and knowledge of liberal arts with products, processes, personnel, and information infrastructure. Convergence innovation in management usually focuses on discarding products with low profitability, cutting down on expenditures, and reducing the workforce in order to make a firm more efficient. However, in order for continuous growth and profitability to be possible, large firms should innovate the three Ps (products, processes, and personnel), information infrastructure systems, and management resources in a systematic, organized, and steady manner. Convergence innovation activity in management faces the following major challenges:

- How to change the business structure in the medium/long term and how to innovate products and services in such a way that competitiveness and value are enhanced in the short term?
- How can a process be optimized to speed up the processing time and reduce the lead time?
- How to innovate regulations and systems in order to make a creative, autonomous, efficient, and speedy organization?
- What should be done to enhance the ability of employees?
- What should be done to build information infrastructure systems for all the processes and organizations within the firm as well as for outside accounts in order to enable the rapid processing of the flow of information, products, and cash on a real-time basis, including the exchange of information, decision making, the exchange of commodities, and payment?
- How to allocate and manage resources in a way that allows changes in the business environment to be met successfully and sustained growth to be facilitated?

It is also imperative to map out an innovation strategy by connecting four targets of innovation to the firm's inherent objectives: profitability, stability, sustainable growth, and contributions to society. Here there is a need to consider profitability as a short-term strategy, stability as a mid-term strategy, and growth as a long-term strategy. It should be emphasized that firms should keep developing new products that can lead the industry, as well as creating new technologies and products that can open new markets in the long term. For this reason, it is of great importance to allocate and manage resources efficiently. Convergence innovation should not be pursued only during times of difficulty. Instead, firms should pursue convergence innovation at all times.

Organizations should perceive a sense of urgency at all times. Organizations tend to be alert during a crisis and make efforts to overcome the crisis. However, during normal times, they are likely to become complacent and disregard necessary preparations for their future. For this reason, a firm that is experiencing normal operations in the present may be facing a dangerous period in the near future. In fact, many industry leaders fall into a bottomless pit after a year or two of high growth and profitability.

3.   Human history and the recognition of a digital revolution

3.1   *Human history through the innovation of science and technology*

Human history has advanced by going through dozens of large-scale paradigm shifts, such as the massive one that is happening currently. To understand the concept of a paradigm shift, it is necessary to understand the role of growth processes in human history. Human history has moved forward each time humans invented tools that led to a more abundant, safer, and more convenient life. The creation of such new lifestyles can be considered a basic human instinct. With the invention of more tools, science and technology have evolved, which in turn has led to the development of new tools. Advances in the production and distribution of tools have led to the establishment of new firms, which in turn have led to the creation of new industries for further economic and social growth.

The driving force behind the advancement of human history involves the invention of tools and the innovation of science and technology, such as the agricultural revolution through primal tools, the industrial revolution through mechanical tools, and the digital revolution through digital tools. Social issues such as government policies, social systems, market demand, and consumer behavior have played crucial roles in the growth of economy and industries. However, from a broader perspective, this growth is fundamentally attributable to the advances in tools and technologies.

3.2   *The Industrial Revolution and changes in core industries*

A brief look at the history of industries in the last 250 years reveals the emergence of new science and technology fields approximately every 50 years, and each time there has been a new source of energy and a new industry. Whenever a new industry was born, there emerged new businesses and entrepreneurs. Some examples include the Industrial Revolution, which started in the United Kingdom at the end of the 1770s; the start of industrialization in the United Kingdom 240 years ago; the beginning of industrialization in the United States 190 years ago; the initiation of industrialization in Germany 160 years ago; and the launch of industrialization in Japan 140 years ago.

Over the years since the Industrial Revolution, leading industries have changed every 50 years: the textile industry at the beginning of the 1800s; railroad/steel industries in the 1850s; automobile, power, and petrochemical industries in the early 1900s; the electronics industry in the 1950s; and the digital industry in the 2000s.

Changes in the leading industries can play crucial roles in the rise and fall of a country and its society and companies. Innovation in science and technology has facilitated multiple shifts from one leading industry to another. Therefore, in order for countries and firms to achieve sustained growth, they should attempt to lead technological innovation or adapt to shifts and trends in the leading industries.

3.3 Recognizing a digital revolution

Recent years have witnessed the rise of a digital revolution based on vast amounts of information and knowledge. In addition, societies themselves have changed rapidly, transforming into knowledge- and information-based societies. Such changes are more striking than before because of a paradigm shift from an industrial society of an analog age to a knowledge- and information-based society of a digital era.

3.3.1 Characteristics of the digital era

First, the digital era can be characterized as an era of rapid technological innovation that has led to sharp declines in prices (see Figure 4.1). Since the 1970s, the degree of integration in the semiconductor field has doubled every 1.5 years. Recently, the degree of semiconductor integration has accelerated, doubling each year. Prices of digital products made by Samsung Electronics have dropped by 40 to 60 percent per year. Therefore, it is difficult to determine an effective strategy for competing with rival firms in a business environment that reflects unlimited competition because of the rapid pace of technological innovation (Bradley et al., 2015).

Second, technological innovation reduces the life cycle of products and fosters heavy competition. For example, it took thirty-five years for radio and fourteen years for TV to attract fifty million users around the globe, whereas it took only four years for the Internet to achieve the same thing. The life cycle of products from their launch to discontinuation is only nine months for monitors and six months for mobile phones.

Third, boundaries between industries have collapsed as a result of intra- and inter-industry convergence, and new competitors have emerged in entirely new

Figure 4.1 Radical changes in the prices of major digital products

types of businesses. Intra-industry convergence means, for example, that the distinction between computers, wired phones, wireless phones, and TV sets has disappeared. Mobile phones are not just tools for telecommunications but also substitutes for cameras, MP3 players, and TV sets. Inter-industry convergence involves the disappearance of the division between such businesses as banks, insurance firms, and security firms. Bancassurance has appeared through the integration of banks and insurance firms. Convenience stores have entered the depository business, and Internet banking has become an integral part of daily life. Broadcasting and telecommunications have converged through IPTV and other services. The development of IT applications and the construction of IT infrastructure systems have led to an era of unlimited competition with no specific business boundaries.

Last, the era of the ubiquitous Internet of Things (IoT) is expected to arrive in the near future, bringing about a new society in which computers are embedded in all things so that communication is possible anytime, anywhere – and all kinds of information and contents are easily shared. An era in which electronic equipment and technologies are key sources of competitive advantage in all industries is expected to emerge in the near future as well. This era is expected to facilitate substantial changes in urban environments, education systems, government systems, national defense, medicine, and logistics.

3.3.2   Lessons

This era of rapid paradigm shifts has two important lessons: (1) changes in the competitive edge and (2) value added in the digital era. First, competitiveness in the analog era came from experience, the accumulation of technologies, and diligence, whereas in the digital era, competitiveness comes from outstanding knowledge, creativity, and speed. Leaders in the analog era had to prioritize vigor and physical capacity over intellectual capacity, whereas those in the digital era must prioritize intellectual capacity over vigor and physical capacity. As for the second implication, the main sources of value added have shifted from manufacturing in the supply chain to core technologies, marketing, and brand value, as well as from sets to core parts and from hardware to software (Joo and Lee, 2010; Yun, 2003).

Without advanced technologies and outstanding individuals, it is difficult to take the initiative in any industry. Technologies tend to serve as a kind of insurance for the future. As for national growth, the source of competitive advantage is outstanding individuals who can lead convergence innovation. Leaders in the digital era require wisdom, insight, and foresight. In a rapidly changing business environment, insight and foresight play crucial roles in predicting changes of the future. To achieve changes, the accumulation of these factors is essential. Leaders should show strong initiative and be passionate about being sources of change. That is, CEOs should have these characteristics and be flexible and open-minded about transforming themselves (Yun, 2007b).

In sum, in the digital era, both early and later movers begin from the same starting line, which can be a challenge as well as an opportunity. In addition, the way in which a firm prepares for its future determines whether it will become a leader or follower in the industry.

4.   Convergence innovation in the management of Samsung Electronics

4.1   *Convergence innovation of Samsung Electronics*

In the 1960s, the Korean economy gained a competitive edge thanks to cheap labor in labor-intensive industries such as lumber, textiles, and shoes, while more advanced countries lost their focus in these industries. Korea's income per capita in the 1960s was a mere $97, whereas that of the Philippines was $250.

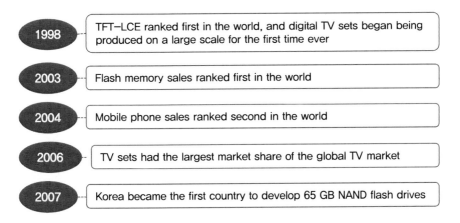

Figure 4.2 Brief history of Samsung Electronics

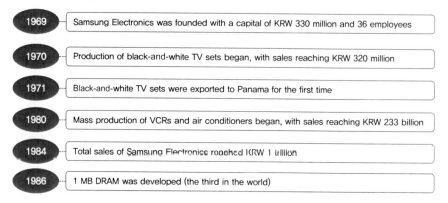

Figure 4.3 Major product innovations at Samsung Electronics

Since the 1990s, the Korean economy has strengthened rapidly in conjunction with the rapid growth of firms that engage in industries like electronic engineering, automobiles, semiconductors, LCDs, and mobile phones. In the 1990s, Korea's GDP was $263 billion, and its per capita income was $6,147.

Samsung Electronics became a leading global firm in just over 30 years. In terms of the number of years taken by firms to reach $80 billion in sales after their foundation, GE took 119 years; IBM, 87 years; and Siemens, 154 years. Samsung Electronics ranked third in the global electronics industry in terms of sales in 2007. Siemens ranked first, followed by HP. In 2004, Samsung Electronics recorded sales of KRW 57 trillion with its profits reaching KRW 800 billion. It was the first time that profits reached the KRW 10 trillion ranges. In 2007, Samsung's exports amounted to $57 billion (see Table 4.1), accounting for 15 percent of Korea's total exports ($370 billion). Also in 2007, Samsung Electronics ranked forty-sixth on the Fortune 500 list, which included fourteen other Korean firms. Walmart ranked first, followed by Exxon (2) and Sony (69). In 2007, Samsung Electronics ranked second in terms of the number of US patents (2,725). IBM ranked first (3,148), followed by Canon, Matsushita Electric, and Intel, in that order. Also in 2007, in terms of brand power, Samsung Electronics ranked twenty-second in all industries (with $16.9 billion). Coca-Cola ranked first, followed by Microsoft (2) and Sony (25).

Samsung Electronics designated the "three Ps" and information infrastructure innovations as its main targets of convergence innovation while it was attempting to establish a more efficient and competitive organization. The first P is product innovation. To cope with changes in the digital era, Samsung Electronics has established business portfolios focused on four major business areas: digital electronics, telecommunications, semiconductors, and LCDs. The company has continued to produce best-selling products in the global market. In order to advance digital convergence, Samsung has also led the convergence of products

Table 4.1 Business performance of Samsung Electronics

Unit: USD trillion

Categories	1997	2000	2007
Related sales	22.5	39.8	92.7
Pretax profits	−0.5	7.9	8.7
Exports	11.1	20.6	57

Source: Samsung Electronics

and the expansion of networks, in addition to dividing businesses into three stages – namely, seeds, seedlings, and fruits.

The second P is process innovation. In today's process innovation, the most important factor is speed, because speed is a crucial component of competitiveness in corporate management. Innovation in the supply chain process aims at the simplest and fastest lead time centered on four mega processes: development management, supply management, customer management, and business management. Innovation in the decision-making process aims to make the process as simple and transparent as possible by reducing steps required to make payments and encouraging online payment methods (Chang, 2012). The main goals of process innovation are to provide products and services to customers in a timely manner and to maximize customer satisfaction by reducing costs. An example of process innovation is the "three-day confirmation system", which enhances the efficiency of production processes. This means that, in accordance with the confirmed schedule, customers place an order to parts suppliers who fulfill the order by a certain deadline. The order is produced that day and shipped on the same date. Through such process innovation, production plans are stabilized, productivity and quality are improved, and costs incurred in the supply process are reduced (Yun, 2007a).

The third P is personnel innovation. Personnel innovation increases the efficiency of an organization and enhances employees' capacity and qualifications. Samsung Electronics has adopted an annual salary system as well as a new evaluation and compensation system (Chang, 2012). It has also adopted the GBM (Global Business Management) system for power transfer and responsible management (Yun, 2007b).

Information infrastructure innovation focuses on enhancing the accuracy and speed of information. In order to exchange information, things, and money simultaneously on a real-time basis, information networks have been built for all global accounts. The information infrastructure of Samsung Electronics is based on ERP and performs demand forecasts and production plans. It includes systems of managing manufacturing sites, technological development, and supplies from subcontractors.

To enable the mutual sharing of necessary information, various systems have been closely linked. Samsung Electronics has built a system with distribution channels so that it can share information on factors such as market demand,

Table 4.2 Investment in the innovation of the information infrastructure at Samsung
Electronics

Categories	Year 2001	Year 2007
IT cost (billion KRW per year)	400	1,000 (increased by 2.5 times)
Number of supporting employees for infrastructure	1,300	2,200 (increased by 900)

Source: Samsung Electronics

customer information, sales figures, and inventories. In this way, it can promptly
supply products, efficiently manage inventories, and quickly respond to customers' needs, which are all important factors that have led to the company's increased
competitiveness. With its accelerated growth and globalization, the information
infrastructure necessary to support the firm has become more complicated, and,
as a result, the amount of its IT investment has increased steadily, reaching KRW
4 trillion over 10 years (see Table 4.2).

4.2   Procedures of convergence innovation

This section discusses Samsung Electronics' convergence innovation procedure
for growth under a rapidly shifting business paradigm. Samsung Electronics has
gone through four convergence innovation stages. The first stage lasted for three
years, from 1997 to 1999. It mainly involved the elimination of "insolvent parts"
by removing marginal businesses and restructuring and removing five ills. The
second stage lasted for two years, from 2000 to 2001. The main aim of that stage
was "building a foundation" for the future by improving manufacturing productivity, building seven processes, and reinforcing an IT infrastructure system.

The third stage lasted for two years, from 2002 to 2003. The slogan of this
stage was "changing organization culture" in order to adapt to the digital paradigm by shifting its focus from manufacturing to development, marketing, and
sales, as well as by completing the company's global SCM and launching the Six
Sigma movement. The fourth stage lasted for four years, from 2004 to 2007.
This stage was a stage for "preparing for the future" to grow into a world leader
by establishing a vision based on relevant ideas and sharing them in an effective
manner. The key contents of convergence innovation in the management of Samsung Electronics can be summarized as follows.

In the wake of the 1997 IMF financial crisis, Samsung Electronics began to
review how it had overcome crises and prepared for the future in the past. In
1995, Samsung Electronics had made a huge profit (USD 3.74 billion in profits
before taxes), the biggest ever since its foundation. For this reason, it had made
reckless investments, such as unplanned overseas expansion, indiscriminative
M&A, holding excessive stock bonds, recklessly spending, and selling products
at preposterously low prices. In summary, it had lax management, which led to
enormous bubbles.

From 1996, however, its business started to be depressed. However, Samsung Electronics was too proud and complacent, believing that it was the number-one company in Korea. A vast organization with eighty-three thousand employees (fifty-eight thousand domestic) could not experience crisis. At that time, it was tainted with a vague hope and illusion that the financial condition would change for the better if economic conditions were to get better and the semiconductor boom were to return.

At the beginning of 1997, some recognized the crisis and initiated a strong innovation program, but the vast organization did not feel the need for change because of pride, carelessness, and complacency. In late 1997, during the IMF crisis in Korea, the company's financial structure deteriorated in the extreme, and its capital was nearly impaired (see Table 4.3). As the IMF financial crisis erupted, Samsung Electronics began to feel a sense of crisis and to realize that it could go bankrupt. It began to see the need for change and innovation, which had been requested for a year. Against this background, strong convergence innovation in management as a whole was initiated in 1997. The first stage was large-scale restructuring to help the company survive in the short run. The second stage was to enhance competitiveness and readiness for the future.

In mid-1998, Samsung Electronics had serious financial difficulty, and its loss amounted to USD 1.4 billion in July. For this reason, it formed an emergency task force to come up with countermeasures and plans. At that time, Samsung concluded that its capital would be completely impaired in two or three years to a level that would cause the company to go belly-up. It also concluded that the company could fail within a year without restructuring. In order to complete restructuring in the shortest amount of time possible, Samsung Electronics chose a strong US-style restructuring in hopes of ensuring its survival, and also conducted a short-term restructuring program in six areas. The biggest concern at that time was how to cope with emotional and physical sacrifice. Innovation and revolution involve some inevitable sacrifice. Samsung had to acknowledge the fact that if employees were not willing to make sacrifices, its innovation efforts

Table 4.3 Business conditions of Samsung Electronics in 1997

Category	Subsidiaries (USD billion)	Head Office (USD billion)
Sales	15.89	13
Profits	340	1.1
Total debt	19.43	12.15 (debt ratio 296%)
Debt	15.19 (foreign debt: 12.2)	93.2 (foreign debt 6.8)
Assets	22.62	16.32
Capital	3.18	4.17
Stocks	2.97	1.63
Bonds	3.25	1.98

Source: Samsung Electronics

would not succeed. A more detailed description of the company's convergence innovation process is as follows:

1   Slimming down manpower and organization: in 1998, a total of twenty-three thousand people, 28 percent of the total number of employees, were laid off.

2   Cutting costs that were neither essential nor urgent: USD 1.24 billion a year. Samsung abolished the bubble benefit package; cut fees for meetings, entertainment, and transportation; pushed ahead with office reform; and outsourced tasks with low added value, such as general affairs, chauffeurs, and vehicle management.

3   Cutting stocks and bonds: stocks and bonds were reduced by USD 2.3 billion in a year from USD 6.2 billion in late 1997 to USD 3.9 billion in late 1998. Cutting down on stocks and bonds was not just for the sake of cost efficiency but also for a change in the quality of management to a virtuous cycle.

4   Selling nonperforming assets: USD 990 million. Icheon Electronics was sold for USD 1.7 billion, real estate for USD 170 million, and golf club memberships. Samsung Electronics also collected employee housing loans worth USD 410 million.

5   Focusing on promising core businesses: Samsung Electronics liquidated 120 businesses that had strong deficits and lacked future potential by exiting the businesses. In particular, the power semiconductor factory in Bucheon was liquidated when future potential was taken into consideration, even though its annual sales were USD 410 million and its profits were USD 80 million. A joint-venture company with GE and HP was sold off, and a defense industry was sold to Thompson.

6   Samsung's financial structure was significantly improved in two years through focus on profit and loss, cash flow, and sound finances. Debt ratio decreased to 85 percent from 300 percent over the same period.

The effects of these restructuring activities appeared after a year and a half, which was faster than had been expected in the latter half of 1999. From that time, Samsung Electronics began to prepare for the future and to enhance its competitive edge by mapping out mid- and long-term strategies. In order to be ready for the future, Samsung Electronics mapped out strategies by acknowledging the reality that as the company entered into the digital age, added value and competiveness, which are the most crucial aspects in management, would have to change as follows: the focus of added value in the supply chain would move from manufacturing to core technology, marketing, and brand power. The added value of products would be transferred to core parts, software, and contents. The competitive edge in the analog era lie in technology, accumulation of experience, and diligence, while in the digital era, it lies in an outstanding brain, creativity, and speed. Samsung Electronics came up with strategies that injected capital into the areas most crucial to added value and competiveness (Yun, 2003).

In the short run, GVE (Group Value Engineering) was executed to cut production costs. This was a campaign intended for productivity reform and market-driven change. Samsung Electronics also formed a task force of one hundred members for convergence innovation, which pushed ahead with SCM, ERP, distribution, and R&D innovation. In the mid-term, by pursuing 3P innovation, Samsung focused on the following six areas (Yun, 2007a):

1   Expanding investment in R&D: Samsung expanded R&D investment to develop core technologies in such areas as semiconductors, LCDs, communication terminals, and systems, as well as digital media products and software. R&D costs increased from KRW 1.2 trillion in 1997 to KRW 2 trillion in 2000 and KRW 5.9 trillion in 2007.

2   Securing an outstanding workforce: an outstanding workforce is one of the most important management resources. Samsung Electronics increased the number of outstanding employees with master's and PhDs, as well as MBA graduates and professional designers (see Table 4.4).

3   Increased investment in facilities: Samsung Electronics made a decisive investment in core parts, including semiconductors and LCDs, which increased from KRW 2.1 trillion in 1997 to KRW 5.4 trillion in 2000 and KRW 10.5 trillion in 2007. For a reference, a comparison can be made with the investment in the Incheon International Airport, which reached KRW 7.8 trillion in eight years and four months.

4   Innovation of the organization and employees: Samsung innovated the organization to adjust to the rapidly changing management environment and make the decision-making process more efficient by introducing a global business management system that makes it possible for a person in charge of a certain business to take care of everything from beginning to end and simplify the organization and approval stages. Moreover, there was innovation in the employees' mindset, such as the recognition of changes and a constant sense of crisis. This was possible by innovating the organizational culture, which promoted voluntary innovation (Chang, 2012).

5   Increased investment in marketing: Samsung Electronics significantly increased marketing expenses from KRW 1.2 trillion in 1997 to KRW 1.8 trillion in 2000 and KRW 5.7 trillion in 2007 by implementing a marketing-oriented strategy which took the main focus off manufacturing.

6   Strengthening education in change management: since the IMF crisis, Samsung has been conducting education in change management for all executives and staff members in three areas – namely, leadership, marketing, and technology. In particular, it has focused on crisis management and change management.

What Samsung Electronics emphasized most in mapping out strategies for the future is that, in the digital era, both front-runners and second movers begin

Table 4.4 Number of employees of Samsung Electronics by educational background

Educational background	1997	2000	2003	2007
R&D work force	13,300	14,100	22,800	39,300
PhD	660	850	2,000	3,680
MA	2,700	3,600	7,200	14,760
MBA (marketing)	30	110	530	650
Designers	260	220	420	780

from the same starting line. For second movers, this serves as both a crisis and an opportunity. Considering that it is a golden opportunity for second movers to outperform front-runners, Samsung has thoroughly prepared for the digital era and focused on enhancing its competitive edge (Yun, 2003). For example, memory semiconductors became a digital product, and mobile phones and TVs changed from analog to digital. If the business environment had not changed from analog to digital, it would have been much more difficult for Samsung Electronics to become the number-one maker of electronic products. In the 1990s, all that Samsung Electronics had to do was just follow in the footsteps of leading companies. However, in order to become a leading global company in the world, Samsung Electronics had to carve out a future path and direction for itself.

5.   Conclusions

5.1   Summary

The case of Samsung Electronics provides important lessons on the convergence innovation of large firms. First of all, it implies that successful innovation must involve the following four processes: (1) Defreezing process: creating a sense of urgency and a sense that a firm cannot survive with existing methods (i.e., creating chaos or denying existing values), existing ways of thinking, and existing behavioral patterns. (2) Organizing process: establishing a clearer vision and objectives and fostering new values, new ways of thinking, and new behavioral patterns. (3) Implementing process: spreading innovation within the organization in an elaborate, concrete, organized, and systematic manner. (4) Freezing process: institutionalizing innovation within the organization. To sum up, a firm's innovation and revolution cannot succeed without a strong sense of crisis, and feeling of a life-or-death struggle. Historically, it has been rare for a firm's innovation and revolution to succeed without a crisis.

In the pursuit of convergence innovation, many hardships can arise, which can become great obstacles to overall innovation activities. The biggest obstacle lies with those who do not want to change. Therefore, leaders themselves must change first. Another problem can arise if there is no sense of urgency in the company. A sense of urgency derives from an accurate understanding of the reality. If a firm has big dreams and objectives, then it is motivated and it perceives a sense of urgency. Habitual routines, stereotyping, egoism, and authoritarianism can also present problems. It is difficult for organizations with the past records of huge success and long history to change.

Another obstacle comes from the resistance from those with vested interests. Those with vested interests want stability and do not welcome changes because any deregulation and institutional innovation means that they may lose their rights. Loss of employees' belief and trust can also be a problem for a company. Innovation involving enormous changes and sacrifices cannot easily succeed without employees' belief and trust.

5.2 Implications

The case of Samsung Electronics provides useful implications for successful convergence innovation in the management of large firms. First, organizations should recognize the importance of courage and patience in coping with the challenges that innovation brings about. Second, they should figure out ways to overcome resistance from people with vested rights. Third, they should plan big objectives and visions for innovation, but make them a reality gradually. Fourth, they should carry innovation forward consistently and continuously. Fifth, they should establish a strong organization to drive innovation. Sixth, they should offer adequate compensation for successful innovation. Last, they should constantly conduct education for all employees on the topics of objectives and visions for changes, as well as a plan for a reaction derived from changes and innovation. Samsung Electronics has the potential to become a leader in technological innovation in the world, and, therefore, it should make all efforts to take advantage of this opportunity, to share its views with concerned individuals and organizations, and to foster success in convergence innovation.

References

Abene, Peter and Newton, Charles (2005), "Technology integration services: Creating convergence", *Chief Learning Officer*, October, pp. 48–52.

Bradley, Steven, Madnick, Stuart and Kim, Changsu (2015), *Digital Business*, Chicago: Chicago Business Press.

Chang, Sug-In (2012), "Study on human resource management in Korea's chaebol enterprise: A case study of Samsung Electronics", *The International Journal of Human Resource Management*, vol. 23, no. 7, April, pp. 1436–1461.

Joo, Si-Hyung and Lee, Keun (2010), "Samsung's catch-up with Sony: An analysis using US patent data", *Journal of the Asia Pacific Economy*, vol. 15, no. 3, August, pp. 271–287.

Yun, Jong-Yong (2003), "Samsung execs outline strategy", *TWICE*, vol. 18, no. 20, September, pp. 9–10.

Yun, Jong-Yong (2007a), *Thinking toward World Premier: Management and Innovation* (in Korean), Suwon: Samsung Electronics.

Yun, Jong-Yong (2007b), *Thinking toward World Premier: History and Future* (in Korean), Suwon: Samsung Electronics.

5 Convergence and diversity in Korea
Moving from catching up to forging ahead

W. Edward Steinmueller

1. Introduction

The Republic of Korea (hereafter, Korea) is one of the few (mostly East Asian) countries to have succeeded over the past several decades in 'catching up' with the levels of productivity and competitiveness associated with 'industrialised nations' in Europe and North America. Ultimately, productivity measures are translated into per capita income, and Korea is now positioned between Spain and Italy in terms of gross national income per capita.[1] In terms of competitiveness, the volume of exports of Korea is comparable with France and the Netherlands.[2] As is often remarked, this is a remarkable achievement. Over several decades of rapid growth, Korea has progressed upward in relative standing from 'middle income' to 'advanced' country status. In this process, Korea has managed to avoid the so-called 'middle income' trap in which the relative standing of a country progresses to the point where increasing wages and declines in the rate of improvement in productivity reduce international competitiveness and slow progress relative to other countries.

Much attention has been devoted to examining the sources of Korea's catching up process (Amsden, 1989; Hobday, 1995). These studies emphasise the significance of a sectoral focus and progress along the now familiar path from being a component supplier to producing systems and, finally, to owning the brand names of systems products. Accompanying these studies is attention to the processes involved in accomplishing catch-up. For example, Linsu Kim emphasised the organisational practices by which technology may be rapidly and effectively assimilated from other countries (Kim, 1999). The significance of sectors and of the intensive effort to assimilate and upgrade technologies in specific sectors is a central message of Keun Lee's study (Lee, 2013). This is one of the several ideas to which we will return in discussing 'post-convergence' growth paths for Korea in the third section of this chapter.

This chapter considers in turn the complexities embedded in the idea convergence in a global and a Korean context, the consequences of pursuing convergence and the alternatives to this goal. It also assesses the changing context in which future economic growth prospects may be sought. A brief conclusion suggests some of the policy implications stemming from these future growth prospects.

2. Catching-up and convergence

'Catching up' is a process with an end; it is possible to catch up with the leaders. Korea has not yet entered the ranks of the highest-income countries and continues, along with virtually all countries, to have segments of the population that have been left behind in the process of rapid growth. Nonetheless, in measures such as those noted above, Korea has entered the ranks of the 'advanced' or wealthy countries. This parity in level of development is sometimes discussed in terms of 'convergence,' a concept that has been discussed for many years, and, hence, it is one that has become layered with several meanings. For example, convergence between the United States and Europe is considered by Scitovsky (1976), who observed that – despite the US post-World War II increase in money income, and hence convergence to European income levels – consumption habits between Europe and the United States have been markedly divergent. Moreover, Europeans, Scitovsky argued, have been enjoying a high quality of life even though they lagged in money income growth. More recently, social scientists have pursued the measurement of 'happiness' in terms of indicators attempting to gauge subjective well-being.[3] Such studies begin with the premise that self-evaluation of life satisfaction is superior to the common economic assumption that income can be translated into utility – in effect, that money can purchase happiness. Although international comparative studies have been conducted for only a few years, it is likely that 'convergence' and 'divergence' are concepts that will be applied to levels of happiness to be observed over time.

More conventionally, convergence has been considered in terms of similarities in patterns of production. Specifically, technological convergence in production is predicated on the idea that there is a global knowledge frontier and that countries and/or industries within countries are located at differing distances from this frontier. Through a process of knowledge acquisition and development over time, countries may move closer to this frontier. Since it is assumed that the frontier advances more slowly than the 'catching up' processes of knowledge acquisition and development, countries necessarily will 'converge,' assuming that they employ (or develop) similar knowledge of production processes. Similarly, the further behind a country is, the greater the possible opportunities for progress and, hence, the faster expected rate of growth. Empirically, convergence through 'catching up' is unusual rather than widespread (Rodrik, 2011a).[4] Historically, related ideas include Vernon (1979), who argued that product- and production-process life cycles involved a process of international diffusion, and Akamatsu (1962), who examined the uneven patterns of diffusion of production in an Asian context. He used the now very familiar 'flying geese' pattern to suggest the presence of a leader-follower relationship in the process of rapid economic development.

This logic of production convergence, somewhat like the traditional assumption of equivalence of income and happiness, is in principle subject to decomposition. For example, the idea of a single knowledge frontier is dubious for a number of areas, food being among the most obvious. More generally, the idea of a common 'best practice' is questionable given the observed diversity, not only in products, but in the underlying variety of capital goods and the production methods employed in their production.[5] To the extent that a common frontier does exist, it may be associated with those industries in which international competition is most intense. This is because small differences in the effectiveness of production processes are likely to be magnified into significant differences in market performance.[6] This reasoning is most applicable to products that are knowledge-intensive – that is, where wage differentials or resource endowments are not a principal source of trade advantage. In addition, the mutual dependence of various processes of production, which may be conducted across firm boundaries, suggests the 'evolution of economic complexity.' This term is used by Hildalgo and Hausmann (2009) to make comparative studies of the composition of exports and imports across countries.

Korea's development has been accompanied by a remarkable shift in the composition of exports. In 1962, Korea's exports were dominated by what are now referred to as resource-based products such as fish and seafood, rice, coal, mining, processed minerals, silk and animal-based products, constituting over two thirds of Korea's exports.[7] By 2013, in contrast, over two thirds of Korea's exports were coming from electronics, machinery (including automobiles), ships and chemicals (including petrochemicals). This transformation in the composition of exports is emblematic of the movement toward capital and knowledge-intensive products which has been closely linked to Korea's overall growth. It has brought Korean companies into more intense competition with leading incumbent companies in wealthier economies.

The composition of Korean exports is an indication of the nature of the country's catching-up process. In order to enter the capital and knowledge-intensive industries, Korea has adopted policies favouring the larger companies organised in Chaebols. The diversified nature of Chaebols provides a large internal capital market that makes it possible to concentrate resources on new initiatives (Chang, 2003). Combined with government strategic funding for specific industries, this form of industrial organisation was well-adapted for the catching-up process. It has allowed rapid scaling up of both physical and human capital resources for industries offering important growth and export opportunities. For example, in shipbuilding, the Korean government and companies identified the large potential for containerised shipping and proceeded to scale up both the size of individual ships and the total ship production. This created a leading global position in the shipbuilding industry and strengthened Korea's steel industry, which, like other countries, has faced enormous competitive pressure (Shin and Ciccantell, 2009).

The relatively high level of aggregation in which machines of all types are considered as a 'sector' despite the very different market characteristics of automobiles, air conditioners, and bulldozers focusses the attention of economists on broadly related industries such as steel. In terms of technological convergence, the diverse demands for steel encouraged diversification of steel production and the development of 'heavy industry' capabilities. These also foster steel applications such as structural steel, military armour (such as the Korean produced XK1 tank) and offshore platforms (latterly for oil exploration and production and, more recently, prospective development for offshore wind farms). This type of development is one of the drivers of technological convergence because acquiring or developing comparable technological means is necessary for meeting diverse requirements.

Finally, it is useful to note the role of standardised consumer goods in driving the technological convergence process. For example, Korea's domestic mobile telephone market, while significant, is far smaller than would be necessary to create an internationally competitive position in this product. In consequence, Korean mobile phone companies have had to develop extensive capabilities in customising mobile phones for overseas markets and mobile telecommunication operators (Park, 2016). It is important, however, to note that they were aided in this process by technologically ambitious Korean mobile operators' efforts to pioneer new 'smartphone' applications (Whang, 2009, 2011). More generally, Korean firms have not only responded to, but also shaped, international consumer goods such as HD (and now UHD) television, air conditioners and other consumer white goods. They have also joined the ranks of major automobile exporters and offshore producers of automobiles. While these examples point towards convergence of domestic and international consumption patterns, there remain areas where Korean domestic demands are truly unique (e.g. the kimchi home refrigerator unit) or are particular to the Korean market (e.g. cuisine more generally).

3.   Consequences of convergence and alternatives

While the catching up and convergence processes described in the previous section have created great benefits, they also have had other consequences. The focus on international competitiveness may leave certain sectors behind. This is a consequence not only of concentration of effort but also of the allocation of capital and labour resources. Notable in this respect is Korea's relatively weak performance in service sector productivity. Catching-up and convergence processes are implicated in Korean service industry performance. As Park and Shin (2012) observe, the rapid shift from the more labour-intensive resource-based industries to the capital- and knowledge-intensive industries was accompanied by very rapid increases in service sector employment, without a corresponding increase in these industries' output. Park and Shin (2012) also observe that information and communication technology (ICT) capital input intensity in Korean service industries is comparatively low (with the exception of telecommunication services). This is remarkable given Korea's strong international position in ICT equipment production and suggests the need for further investigation.

A possible explanation for this outcome is that the export-growth of the ICT industries has outbid service industry employers for personnel with complementary skills needed for more intensive use – and, hence, investment – in ICTs. There may also be an important gender issue. Despite some improvement, Korea has the highest median wage differential between men and women of OECD countries (OECD, 2016). In the last decade (2004–2014), male employment in manufacturing has increased by 11 percent while female manufacturing employment has declined by the same percentage (OECD, 2016). Correspondingly, male service industry employment has increased by 19 percent in this decade while female service industry employment has increased by 26 percent. The increasing capital and knowledge intensity of manufacturing is accompanied by displacement of women (being paid lower wages on average) into services, reducing pressure to make capital investments (such as in ICT systems) in the service industry. This short examination of Korean service industry productivity issues is not offered as a complete explanation of Korean service sector productivity lags, but it is an indication that rapid catch-up processes have consequences beyond the overall improvement in economic growth which has been a central focus in Korea's public and industrial policies. The service sector is only one, though the largest, of the sectors to have experienced problematic consequences as a result of the catching-up process.

A second set of consequences relates to the fates of the industries that have become dominant in the catching-up process. As Lee (2013) notes, these industries are characterised by 'rapid cycles' – that is, rapid scaling up of new products and production methods, and the necessity of continuing an intense effort to maintain an internationally competitive position. While commitment to these industries creates a salutatory industrial discipline, it is not without hazard. Examples of such industries include mobile phones and personal computers, both of which have experienced precipitous changes in global market share for producer countries over the past two decades. This highlights the fact that a 'catching up' growth pattern might not involve a broader pattern of technological convergence. Of course, another way of describing this is to say that 'catching up,' particularly if it occurs over a relatively short period of time and involves an export-led growth strategy, may lead to specialisation. Whether described as a lack of technological convergence or as specialisation, the possibility exists that with a narrower base, economies in this position may be subject to greater risk if they are unable to retain or enlarge their market shares in those industries in which they are relatively specialised.

Lee (2013) argues that development prescriptions urging diversification and greater technological convergence may be premature if the greatest opportunities or capabilities exist in specialisation strategies. This argument poses two related questions. First, is convergence (i.e. diversification from Korea's current position) inevitable? Second, even if it is not inevitable, does diversification offer a desirable trade-off between risk and returns from specialisation? As noted previously, the catching-up process may leave particular sectors behind in terms of productivity improvement. The consequence of this is that greater opportunities to improve productivity may exist outside the specialised sectors than within them. Whether this will lead to investment re-allocation, however, is an empirical issue. The answer is partially shaped by Korean public policies, which, as noted, have favoured the larger domestic manufacturing companies. The example of services also highlights the potential limits to this re-allocation process. In other industries, improvements might be expected from foreign direct investment.[8]

The variety of industries that experiences growth as a result of income elasticities (as Koreans reach higher incomes and the demand for these industries' outputs increases) would suggest that some degree of convergence is inevitable, but this may be substantially delayed by government policies.

Ultimately, the extent to which Korean public policymakers wish to trade off medium-term risk over the advantages of specialisation is a political choice. It may be argued that, because specialisation offers substantial short- and medium-term benefits including important positive fiscal and social welfare consequences from this growth, it might be continued indefinitely or until the risks are realised as realities.

4.　Moving toward diversity

The means by which diversification might be fostered in the Korean economy is examined in this section. This discussion is guided by historical examples of the catching-up process and by contemporary observations about diversification processes in other advanced economies. As the previous section concluded, some degree of diversification is likely although there is a credible case in favour of maintaining specialisation.

In considering features of catching-up that are seen as barriers to future diversification and the common exploration by advanced economies of the technological frontier, discussion often begins with the nature of 'imitation,' the ability to follow quickly and efficiently leads taken elsewhere. Over two decades ago, we attempted to invert this discussion by considering the question of why Americans were such poor imitators (Rosenberg and Steinmueller, 1988). We observed that the process of imitation not only involved considerable technological capability, but also that innovation following incumbent firms' leadership is a futile strategy if the incumbents' products or prices cannot be improved upon. Of course, in the process of economic development there is a narrow window of time during which the skills and capabilities necessary for imitation can be assembled while the wage level still offers advantages. This window may have existed for Korea in the twentieth century, but it is no longer a very important factor. Indeed, even the vast reservoir of under-employed and lower-wage labour in China that has driven that economy's growth performance is rapidly coming to an end. Achieving an advanced country position may involve imitation, but this process also entails mastery of the capacity to make process (cost saving and quality improving) innovations and frequently involves important incremental product innovations as well.

The issue of which direction will further Korean growth turns on the balance between deepening and extending existing capabilities and the undertaking of fundamentally new activities where little prior experience (either imitative or inventive) has been accumulated. Moreover, these choices for the future are also influenced by the contemporary context in which the accumulation of greenhouse gasses (GHG) has introduced stark new constraints on the direction of growth and the nature industrial output. These constraints are, nevertheless, also opportunities for future growth.

The capabilities built during the catching-up process can be employed in a variety of ways to develop new markets and products. For example, capabilities in electronics which are currently deployed in the rapid cycle sectors of mobile phones and personal computers are applicable to the production of smart grid, smart home and smart city applications. Each of these application areas may, in principle, contribute to sustainability (the reduction of GHG emissions and more efficient use of materials as well as energy). However, the frontier nature of these industry specialisations has yet to yield the aggregate market size or rate of growth of other electronic equipment or service markets. The reasons for this are largely related to the retro-fitting of older systems that are unlikely to be entirely rebuilt in the short run. A new collection of standards and practices is likely to arise in each of these areas. There is considerable risk that these standards will be fragmented, delaying the growth of markets and, ultimately, the contribution that 'smart' capabilities in energy production and distribution for homes and cities can make to sustainability.[9] What this suggests is that Korean firms and the government need a process of capability building with regard to both standards making processes and the complex requirements of such systems. This may also be an area where international collaboration with other companies extends the existing capabilities of Korean firms.

Another set of 'extending' activities involves building capabilities that are complementary to existing specialisations. For example, there are a number of Korean logistics companies that offer global services. Extension of these activities in combination with the continued building of containerised shipping offers opportunities for extending and integrating the shipping, tracking and logistics fulfilment activities. As the Korean International Logistics Council notes, the current profile of logistics in Korea is oriented toward shipping in a global context of supply chain integration which requires an extensive array of specialised services.[10] Complementary capabilities are also significant in many other areas. They often extend into service provision which requires both more extensive internationalisation of business practice and the use of modern ICT capacities. These are areas that differ from large-scale manufacturing activities which have been central in catching up.

A number of areas are at the boundary between extension and deepening and new activities. These include the development of the 'creative industries,' a broad category of activities that is defined in many different ways. Some of these definitions are helpful insofar as they do not exclude industries such as those involving artisans and artists. Perhaps the most useful definition for the present discussion is those industries where the 'creative content' involves substantial 'reproducible' information. This is because there are inherent economies of scale in reproducing information – while first copy costs are substantial, marginal costs in such activities are very low. If competitive products can be produced, they will be very profitable. Examples of information-based creative industries include software, media and industrial design. A key feature of these activities is that part of the internationalisation process which accommodates the diversity of localised demands. The creative industries also involve different cultural norms than manufacturing. While manufacturing involves a degree of regimentation in following routines in order to maintain quality and reliability, the information-based creative industries involve a greater degree of non-conformity or even eccentricity which allows individual creators the scope to realise original visions and designs (Florida, 2004). In these industries, greater variety is often necessary to market test innovations before large-scale production and distribution can occur. Korean companies have substantial technological knowledge about the platforms used to convey the results of creative industry activities. Producing the content for these platforms, however, is a challenge that requires cultivating different cultural norms and practices. It thus involves important departures from the activities of refinement and incremental innovation on existing technologies.

Finally, there are areas of development in which Korea has not yet achieved a strong international position. Many of these are science-based industries such as pharmaceuticals, scientific instruments, nanotechnology and biotechnology. Success in the science-based industries involves pioneering at the frontier rather than catching up, and new markets often have to be built for major innovations. For example, in addition to the uncertain costly process of discovery and the expensive process of clinical trials, new pharmaceuticals have to be marketed to physicians throughout the world, an activity that brings its own demands for internationalisation and market presence. In addition, virtually all of the advanced economies have set goals to become even more science-based and have built large scientific infrastructures in support of this aim. This is not to discount Korea's prospects in these areas but instead to suggest that science-based industry development is subject to over-subscription. For example, virtually every advanced economy has a programme in biotechnology despite the relatively modest revenues generated by this industry so far. These industries offer an unusually diverse set of demands and markets and the demonstrated capabilities of Korean firms to identify emergent possibilities and move quickly to commercially exploit them can be a significant advantage. However, it is also the case that participation in these industries is subject to experience-based development. In order to have the absorptive capabilities (Cohen and Levinthal, 1990) needed to identify these opportunities, some prior experience is needed. Korean efforts in these areas are worth monitoring. Considerable support for early development can be offered by the large number of Korean government research institutes (such as KIST) and by large-company-based and university-based research institutes. In this respect, Korea has a well-developed science and technology system that appears to be somewhat constrained by a focus on short-term company-oriented research needs.

In summary, a strategy of greater diversification remains an option as a response to the risk associated with the current dominance of the catching-up industries and the uneven inter-sectoral performance exemplified by the service sector. Such a diversification strategy should not be undertaken for its own sake – that is, to make the Korean economy more closely resemble one or another of the wealthier economies in the OECD. Those economies also face risks associated with their 'me too' strategies towards science-based development, and many face their own diversification problems as the result of precipitous deindustrialisation over the past several decades. There are, however, some common elements in the diversification options available, and these provide the basis for the following conclusion.

5. Conclusions

The common element in most of the strategic diversification options suggested in the previous section is 'internationalisation.' This is, of course, not a new subject in the Korean context. In order to achieve the success of an export-led growth strategy, Korean firms have mastered many of the elements necessary for a global strategy. There is, however, an important difference between exporting innovative mass-produced products or large-scale capital goods such as ships and many of the product and service markets identified as options for Korean diversification. This difference is in the degree of localisation required to adapt goods and services for different markets and for cultural differences. With Korean firms faced with the steady rise in capabilities of Chinese companies to produce the same goods that have been responsible for Korea's historical success, it seems important for Korean firms to re-assess the nature and extent of their capabilities with regard to a deeper internationalisation of their products and services. To do so will require an intensification of outward-looking strategies and engagements. This will also require important changes in Korean social and educational capabilities.

The skills necessary for catching-up are not the same as those required for a deeper process of the internationalisation of Korea's position. While Korea has demonstrated world-class capability in producing engineers and managers, the consequence of this focus is a common subject of commentary in Korea. 'Too much attention to narrow problem-solving' or 'too little creativity and expression in schools' typify the comments made by students and observers of Korean education. For Korea to exploit the emerging options now that it has reached the frontier, a deeper degree of internationalisation of education seems desirable.

The theme of more extensive internationalisation is also significant with regard to scepticism about future possibilities of developing countries to follow Korea's example of rapid industrialisation. If catching up and convergence are now more difficult as the result of globalisation, Korea may play an important role in fostering late industrialisation in other countries. In particular, the accumulation of experience in adapting and re-configuring capital goods, building worker skills from relatively low levels and identifying export opportunities are all capabilities that are exportable as services and in furtherance of Korea's position as a major international actor.

With an increased focus on internationalisation, emerging opportunities for extending and deepening Korea's existing capabilities in new markets (such as those in the energy field provided by smart grids, smart homes and smart cities or further development of international logistics operations as a key service industry for seeking productivity improvements) can be better exploited. Further internationalisation will also open up opportunities in the information-based creative industries. These would complement and extend existing Korean capabilities in building the ICT platforms and infrastructures. Finally, deeper participation in science and science-based industries is intrinsically an activity compatible with promoting and producing greater internationalisation. The pursuit of frontier building is an international activity in which elements of cooperation and competition co-exist and from which all participants are able to recognise new opportunities for growth, prosperity and sustainability.

Notes

1 According to the World Bank rankings based upon purchasing power parity for 2014; see World Bank, International Comparison Program database at http://data.worldbank.org/ (last accessed 24 January 2016).
2 UN Trade Tables at http://unstats.un.org/unsd/trade/data/tables.asp (last accessed 24 January 2016).
3 For a starting point to the large literature on this subject and a recent implementation, see Helliwell, Layard and Sachs (2015).
4 Rodrik takes a pessimistic view of the prospects for developing countries based upon an analysis of the globalisation process which he argues removes possibilities for later industrialisation (Rodrik, 2011b) and, more recently, empirical observation of a peak in industrial employment occurring at ever lower per income capita levels in developing countries (Rodrik, 2015).
5 A more complete analysis of this line of thought is Gertler (2001), who uses and critiques the term 'best practice' to consider the possibilities for 'strong convergence' – i.e. similarities in production process.
6 In this regard, it is also important that the global production of capital goods is relatively concentrated with 80 percent of the value of such goods being produced in eight countries (Eaton and Kortum, 2001). The assumption here is that, outside of resource-based exports, the capital goods used in producing exports are at least and probably more concentrated in their origins.
7 Calculated from (Simoes, Landry, Hildago et al., 2016) a 1962 visualisation for Korea at http://atlas.media.mit.edu/en/visualize/tree_map/sitc/export/kor/all/show/1962/ (last accessed 25 January 2016).
8 For example, Lee, Hong and Sun (2014) provide limited evidence concerning the positive effects of FDI on Korean domestic firm formation although it does not address sector differences.
9 Smart homes and cities have many other facets than energy efficiency. However, the critical application that is likely to drive these other facets are efficiencies in energy and materials use.
10 See http://kilc.kita.org/kilc_org/logistics/logistics01.jsp (last accessed 30 January 2016).

References

Akamatsu, K. (1962), "A historical pattern of economic growth in developing countries", *Journal of Developing Economies*, vol. 1, no. 1, pp. 3–25.

Amsden, A. (1989), *Asia's Next Giant: South Korea and Late Industrialization*, Oxford: Oxford University Press.

Chang, S.-J. (2003), *The Rise and Fall of Chaebols*, Cambridge: Cambridge University Press.

Cohen, W. and D. A. Levinthal (1990), "Absorptive capacity: A new perspective on learning and innovation", *Administrative Science Quarterly*, vol. 35, no. 1, pp. 128–152.

Eaton, J. and S. Kortum (2001), "Trade in capital goods", *European Economic Review*, vol. 45, pp. 1195–1235.

Florida, R. (2004), *The Rise of the Creative Class: Revisited*, New York: Basic Books.

Gertler, M. S. (2001), "Best practice? Geography, learning and the institutional limits to strong convergence", *Journal of Economic Geography*, vol. 1, no. 1, pp. 5–26.

Helliwell, J., R. Layard and J. Sachs (eds.) (2015), *World Happiness Report 2015*, New York: Sustainable Development Solutions Network.

Hildalgo, C. A. and R. Hausmann (2009), "The building blocks of economic complexity", *Proceedings of the National Academy of Sciences*, vol. 106, no. 26, pp. 10570–10575.

Hobday, M. (1995), *Innovation in East Asia: The Challenge to Japan*, Cheltenham: Edward Elgar.

Kim, L. (1999), *Learning and Innovation in Economic Development*, Cheltenham: Edward Elgar.

Lee, K. (2013), *Schumpterian Analysis of Economic Catch-Up: Knowledge, Path Creation and the Middle Income Trap*, Cambridge: Cambridge University Press.

Lee, I. H., E. Hong and L. Sun (2014), "Inward foreign direct investment and domestic entrepreneurship: A regional analysis of new firm creation in Korea", *Regional Studies*, vol. 48, no. 5, pp. 910–922.

OECD (2016), *Labour Force Statistics*, Paris: OECD (http://stats.oecd.org/Index.aspx?DataSetCode=STLABOUR).

Park, D. U. (2016), *Latecomer Firms and Pursuit of a Dual Frontier: The Case of Korean Handset Manufacturers*, PhD Dissertation, Brighton: University of Sussex.

Park, D. and K. Shin (2012), *Performance of the Service Sector in the Republic of Korea: An Empirical Investigation*, Manila: Asia Development Bank.

Rodrik, D. (2011a), "The future of economic convergence", *NBER Working Papers*, no. 17400, pp. 1–48.

Rodrik, D. (2011b), *The Globalization Paradox: Democracy and the Future of the World Economy*, New York and London: W.W. Norton.

Rodrik, D. (2015), "Premature deindustrialization", *Journal of Economic Growth*, vol. 21, no. 1, pp. 1–33.

Rosenberg, N. and W. E. Steinmueller (1988), "Why are Americans such poor imitators?", *American Economic Review*, vol. 78, no. 2, pp. 229–234.

Scitovsky, T. (1976), *The Joyless Economy: An Inquiry into Human Satisfaction and Consumer Dissatisfaction*, New York: Oxford University Press.

Shin, K.-H. and P. S. Ciccantell (2009), "The steel and shipbuilding industries of South Korea: Rising East Asia and globalization", *Journal of World-Systems Research*, vol. 15, no. 2, pp. 167–192.

Simoes, A., D. Landry, C. Hildago, and M. Teng (2016), "Observatory of economic complexity" (http://atlas.media.mit.edu/en/).

Vernon, R. (1979), "The product cycle hypothesis in a new international environment", *Oxford Bulletin of Economics and Statistics*, vol. 41, no. 4, pp. 255–267.

Whang, Y. K. (2009), *Convergence, Capabilities and Complexity: The Case of the Mobile Handset Industry in Korea*, PhD Dissertation, Brighton: University of Sussex.

Whang, Y. K. (2011), "Local 'test bed' market demand in the transition to leadership: The case of the Korean mobile handset industry", *World Development*, vol. 39, no. 8, pp. 1358–1371.

Part III

Convergence innovation in Asian countries and industries

6 Sector and country differences in convergence innovation

Comparisons with Korea, China, Japan, and Taiwan

Kong-rae Lee and Guktae Kim

1. Introduction

Convergence innovation is here defined as 'a horizontal and vertical integration of diverse technologies creating new products, processes, and services'. Horizontal integration means an absorption of diverse fields of technologies for the purpose of creating new functions and products, which often broadens the scope of their technological specialization that can interact with partner companies or individuals. Vertical integration means deepening of specific technologies connecting technological fields of forward and backward sectors for the purpose of creating new functions and products.

Modern innovations have had a strong tendency of technological convergence in which information and telecommunication technology plays a central role as it has been applied to vast areas of industries, generating a variety of new products and services. Not only IT technologies but also other technologies are converging or being converged at varying degrees of integration, routinely creating intellectual property rights. The phenomenon of convergence innovation is likely to even deepen and widen in the future due to intense competition among firms in global markets. Particularly, manufacturing firms in Asian countries have been active in convergence innovation that has led a revolution of the world industries.

Looking back on the history of technological innovation as Rosenberg (1963, 1982) found, the phenomenon of convergence innovation emerged at the end of the nineteenth century as closely related technological problems were solved and shared among manufacturers of different types of metal-processing machines. Machines confronted a similar collection of technological problems dealing with such matters as power transmission, control devices, feed mechanisms, friction reduction, and a broad array of problems connected with the properties of metals. These problems became common to the production of a wide range of commodities. These were apparently unrelated from the point of view of the nature of the final product. The uses, however, of the final product were very closely related on a technological basis. Rosenberg called this phenomenon 'technological convergence' and argued that the intensive degree of specialization which developed in the second half of the nineteenth century owed its existence to a combination of this technological convergence.

Since the concept of 'technological convergence' appeared at the end of the nineteenth century, similar terminologies have been developed by relatively few innovation scholars such as Kodama (1986, 1991, 1994) and Kong-rae Lee and Jung-tae Hwang (2005), and Kong-rae Lee (2007, 2015). They argued that convergence innovation is a fundamental phenomenon prevailing in the modern industries and that it is associated with strong leadership in a particular technology, and can be possible through concerted efforts by several technological experts. Convergence innovation has contributed not only to the rapid growth of companies but also to the gradual growth of all the companies in many industries (Lee and Hwang, 2005).

This paper aims to measure the degree of convergence innovation and their trends at the industry level. The data set used is composed of twelve years of data in longitude from five industry types with thirty-nine sub-industry sectors and comparisons of four countries having patent applications in the United States: Japan, Korea, Taiwan, and China. This paper measured intra-industry convergence and inter-industry convergence in the case of the Korean industries and made a convergence innovation matrix based on the results of the analysis. We hope that this study will provide a clue to exploring further the structure of convergence innovation at the meso and macro level. Innovation studies that focused on convergence innovation need to deepen their framework toward various perspectives in the future.

The outline of this paper is as follows. Section 2 explains research methods and data for this study. Section 3 analyzes innovation trends of the Korean industries in terms of patenting activities in the United States. Section 4 investigates industry differences in making convergence innovation. Intra-industry convergence, inter-industry convergence and convergence innovation matrix are defined and those of the Korean industry are measured. Section 5 analyzes country differences in intra-industry and inter-industry convergence innovation among four Asian countries: China, Japan, Korea, and Taiwan. Section 6 provides concluding remarks.

2.   Research methods and data

2.1   *Classification of industry types*

Classification of industries based on their characteristics of innovation has been often used for analyzing innovation issues. A number of innovation studies (OECD, 1993; Pavitt, 1984, 1992; Tidd, Bessant and Pavitt, 2001) have shown similar and persistent differences amongst industries in the sources and direction of technological innovation. The four types of industrial taxonomy made by Pavitt (1984) have been well known and have been applied to many innovation studies. Tidd et al. (2001) developed Pavitt's taxonomy and applied it to the classification of firms. They classified five types of industries or firms (supplier dominated, scale-intensive, science based, information intensive, and specialized suppliers) based upon technological trajectories which were originally conceived by Pavitt.

We adopted Tidd's typology on the types of firms and applied it to classification of industry types. They are supplier dominated, information intensive, specialized suppliers, scale intensive, and science based. This typology deems to be useful to understand the degree of convergence within an industry type, which can be called intra-industry convergence, or between industry types, which can be called inter-industry convergence. Convergence trends in those five industry types may reveal many implications for the innovation of Korean industries.

There is one thing worth mentioning regarding industrial classification. The traditional concept of distinction between firm and industry is in fact ambiguous since some of the large firms run their business across many industrial sectors. For instance, Samsung Electronics Co. has operated its business across many industrial sectors: semiconductors, information, mobile telecommunications, displays, home appliances, and digital media. Some scholars like Fujimoto (2007) equally treated firms and industries in innovation research. He argued that the lowest level of micro unit analysis is not firm but factory. This paper hereafter adopts the typology of five industry types by which firms and specific industries are grouped and analyzed as shown in Table 6.1.

2.2 Data

US patent statistics have been used for a proxy of innovation. It well represents an upstream part of the innovation cycle that includes such inventions as new ideas, prototypes of new products, new processes, and new designs. It is, however, not able to account for the degree of utilization, industrial difference of propensity to

Table 6.1 Classification of products and services by industry types

Types	Specific products and services
Supplier dominated (Sd)	food processing (beverages, food stuffs, cigarettes, etc.), textiles, metal products, glass and ceramics, non-ferrous metal, lighting instruments, etc.
Information intensive (Ii)	audio instruments, telecom instruments, office instruments, other services, etc.
Specialized suppliers (Ss)	engines, agricultural machinery, construction and mine machinery, machine tools, special industrial machinery, general industrial machinery, service industrial machinery, transmission instruments, electrical industrial machinery, home appliances, electronic parts, weaponry, shipbuilding, railroad equipment, etc.
Scale intensive (Si)	petro chemicals, inorganic and organic chemicals, paint, rubbers, plastics, iron and steels, TV, automobiles, other transportation equipment, etc.
Science based (Sb)	pharmaceuticals, oils and cosmetics, agro chemicals, other chemicals, precision instruments, aerospace and aircrafts

patent, and some kinds of innovation results such as software, trade secrets, and know-how associated with production processes. This paper supposes that those industries with high shares in the US patents have a leading position especially in the upstream part of the innovation cycle.

The time horizon of the data is twelve years, from 2001 to 2012. The data set is composed of twelve years of data in longitude from five industry types with thirty-nine sub-industry sectors. It has also drawn data of four countries having patent applications in the US: Japan, Korea, Taiwan, and China. Our data set has three dimensions such as sectoral, time series, and countries. This data enabled us to adopt a comprehensive archival analysis for discovering sectoral differences in convergence innovation.

2.3   Method to measure CIs

The method to measure the degree of convergence innovation (CI) is to calculate the percentage of patents with more than one USPTC class citation in technology fields out of the total number of patents in an industry. Two types of convergence innovation can be measured. One is intra-industry convergence, in which technologies converge within an industry sector; the other is inter-industry convergence, in which a technology converges with other technology fields which belong to other industry sectors. It is assumed that frequent occurrences of patents with more than one USPTC class citation indicate a high degree of convergence innovation.

$$CI_{ijt} = \sum_{1}^{ijt} \frac{CP_{ijt}}{P_{ijt}} \qquad (1)$$

The degree of convergence innovation can be expressed as equation (1) where CP_{ijt} indicates convergence patents with more than one USPTC class citation in technology field I in industry j at time period t and where P_{ijt} indicates the number of patent applications in technology field i in industry j. Convergence patents are defined as patents with more than one USPC class citation. CI_{ijt} is a converted percentage index representing the degree of convergence innovation in technology field i, in industry j, and at time period t. The time period here is twelve years, from 2001 to 2012. Intra-industry CI is obtained by limiting j to a specific industry so as to measure CI within the industry. Inter-industry CI is obtained by counting convergence patents that hold more than one USPTC class citation pending on two industries (j). In calculating the inter-industry CI, we made ten pairs of industrial types (Sd-Ii, Sd-Ss, Sd-Si, Sd-Sb, Ii-Si, Ii-Si, Ii-Sb, Ss-Si, Ss-Sb, and Si-Sb).

3.   Innovation trends of Korea by industrial type

The results of US patent analysis across five industry types revealed that the specialized suppliers of Korea took the largest share of US patents. The industry includes engine, agricultural machinery, construction and mine machinery, machine tools, various industrial machinery, electrical machinery, home appliances, electronic parts, weaponry, shipbuilding, railroad equipment, and so forth. In 2001, its US patent share was 6.1 percent, which increased to 14.7 percent in 2012. The information-intensive industry, such as audio instruments, telecom instruments, office instruments, and so forth, followed the specialized suppliers, accounting for 3.5 percent of US patents in 2001, which also substantially increased to 6.9 percent in 2012. These two types of industries have actually led the innovation of Korean industries and the growth of the Korean economy. On average, the Korean industries took 8.5 percent of the total US patents in 2012, which has been continuously increasing.

Except for the two industries, three other types of industries have shown a rather stagnant trend in patenting activities in the United States or slightly declining over the last twelve years as seen in Figure 6.1. The science-based industry, such as pharmaceuticals, oils and cosmetics, chemicals, precision instruments, and aerospace and aircrafts, showed almost identical patterns with that of the scale intensive industry that has been traditionally a strategic sector of Korea. The suppliers-dominated industry – such as food processing (beverages, food stuffs, cigarettes, etc.), textiles, metal products, glass and ceramics, non-ferrous metal, lighting instruments, and so forth – accounted for the smallest portion in US patent applications.

As seen in Figure 6.2, patenting of the Korean industries in the United States revealed a downturn trend from 2008 during the year the monetary crisis began in the United States. Since then, it tends to recover shortly in 2010 and reveals a downturn again from 2012. The trends of patenting activities in the United States are overall in accordance with economic trends of Korea. This implies that innovation of the Korean industry has influenced or been influenced by general trends of economic activities in Korea.

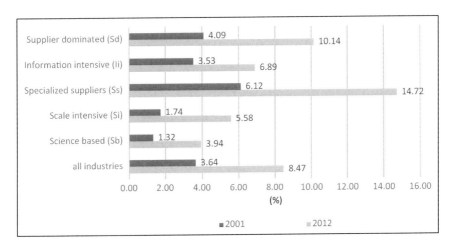

Figure 6.1 Changes in US patent shares of Korea by industry type

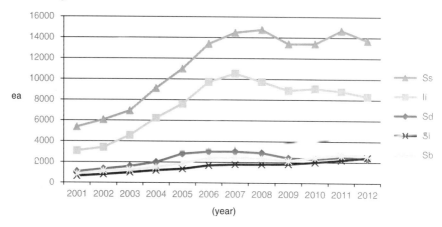

Figure 6.2 Patenting trends of Korea in the United States by industrial type

Note: Symbols of graphic lines denote as follows – Ss (specialized suppliers), Ii (information-intensive firms), Si (scale-intensive firms), Sb (science-based firms), and Sd (supplier-dominated firms)

If we see the US patent shares of specific industries, it is found that the Korean shipbuilding industry that showed the largest global export market share ironically obtained extremely low level of US patents. The industry accounted for just 0.3 percent of US patents in 2001, which tends to decrease over time. Some managers of a shipbuilding company said that the industry keeps technological innovations a secret for protection rather than patenting because they are mostly associated with processes of shipbuilding which are less likely to be protected by a patent law when infringed by a third party (Lee and Rhee, 2008).

4.   Industry differences in convergence innovation

4.1   *Intra-industry differences*

According to a study on the technological innovation of textile machinery (Lee, Yun and Jeong, 2015), convergence innovation takes place mainly when a firm enters into new industrial areas based on their core competences. Firms having a core competence in some technology field tend to endeavor to make outside-in or inside-out type convergence innovation depending on the market situation. When a firm loses market share in a core competence area, the firm tries to apply it to the innovation of new products and processes, which can help enter into new markets. This is called an inside-out type of convergence innovation. Conversely, a firm that gains competitive advantage in core competence areas tends to actively apply outside technologies to innovate new products and services in its own competence areas. This is called an outside-in type of convergence innovation.

Are the trends of such convergence innovation the same or different by industrial sectors? Let us look at overall trends of convergence innovation taking place

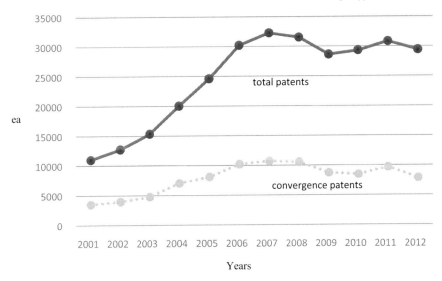

ea

Figure 6.3 Trends of convergence patents of Korea in the United States

in Korea over the last twelve years before looking at the sector level trends. Figure 6.3 illuminates overall trends of convergence patents of Korea. At first sight, its trend has been in line with that of total US patents. However its shares out of total patents are declining over time from 31.8 percent in 2001, to 30.6 percent in 2008, and to 26.9 percent in 2012. These trends imply that convergence innovation of the Korea industry has not been much changed at all. Is it really so? Looking at the trends at the meso level may help answer this question.

In order to scrutinize the trends of convergence innovation at the meso level, we calculated two kinds of convergence as previously mentioned: intra-industry convergence and inter-industry convergence. Intra-industry convergence is defined as the percentage share of convergence patents with more than one IPC class citation in technology fields within an industry sector. As the results of calculating intra-industry convergence, we obtained graphical results as shown in Figure 6.4. Surprisingly the specialized suppliers sector has taken the greatest degree of intra-convergence innovation, fluctuating from 40 percent to 50 percent out of total patents. It implies that diverse machinery has been rapidly innovating by converging outside technologies, particularly IT technology or being converged.

The second industry revealing a high degree of convergence innovation has been taking place in the information-intensive industry. We expected that this industry may have the greatest degree of convergence innovation because of exploiting technological opportunities created by the emergence of innovative information and telecommunication technology. However, the reality does not show such trends. There have been relatively active convergence innovations in the information-intensive industry, but remaining around the 30 percent level. Moreover, it has a rather declining tendency as shown in Figure 6.4. The information-intensive

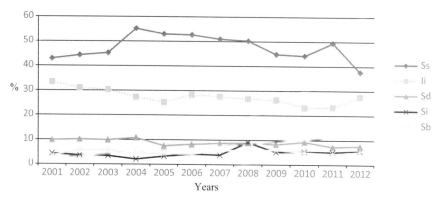

Figure 6.4 Trends of intra-industry convergence of Korean industries

Note: Symbols of graphic lines denote as follows – Ss (specialized suppliers), Ii (information intensive), Si (scale intensive), Sb (science based), and Sd (supplier dominated)

industry seems to play a role of infrastructural technology in the innovation of vast areas of the manufacturing industry due to its application to vast industrial areas.

The other three sectors, such as the scale-intensive, the science-based, and the supplier-dominated industries, do not show an impressive trend. The supplier-dominated industry – including food processing, textiles, metal products, glass and ceramics, non-ferrous metal, lighting instruments, and so forth – has showed a medium degree of convergence innovation revealing around 10 percent over the period. The other two industries showed even lower than that of the supplier-dominated industry with less than 10 percent. The scale-intensive and the science-based industries are actually important for the Korean economy to create and build up the next-generation industries to increase the potential growth rate of the Korean economy.

4.2   Inter-industry differences

Turning to inter-industry convergence innovation, Figure 6.5 reveals the trends of inter-industry convergence of the Korean industries. The degree of inter-industry convergence is calculated as the percentage share of convergence patents with more than one USPTC class citation between technology fields that belong not to their own industry sector but to other industry sectors. There are ten pairs of inter-industry convergences (Si-Sb, Ss-Si, Ss-Sb, Ii-Ss, Ii-Si, Ii-Sb, Sd-Ss, Sd-Si, Sd-Sb, and Sd-Ii) since there are five industrial sectors. As the result of calculating ten pairs of inter-industry convergence, we obtained graphical results as shown in Figure 6.5.

The greatest inter-industry convergence appeared in the pair of Si-Sb (the scale intensive and the science based). It is assumed that scale-intensive firms like motor companies having a huge scale of smart manufacturing systems have actively achieved convergence innovations for equipping their competent production systems. The next is followed by the convergence innovations between

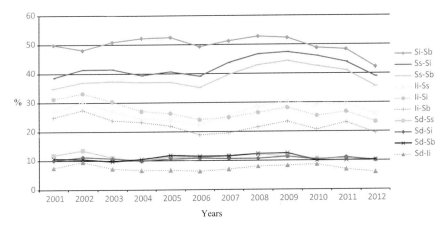

Figure 6.5 Trends of inter-industry convergence of Korean industries

Note: Symbols of graphic lines denote as follows – Ss (specialized suppliers), Ii (information-intensive firms), Si (scale-intensive firms), Sb (science-based firms), and Sd (supplier-dominated firms).

the specialized suppliers and the scale intensive (Ss-Si) and between the specialized suppliers and the science based (Ss-Sb). This tendency implies that the machinery industry has been a focal industry of convergence innovation adopting forward industries (for instance, the automobile industry as a representative scale-intensive sector) and backward industries (for instance, the precision instrument industry as a representative science-based sector).

Inter-industry convergence between the information-intensive industry and other industries did not take place much. It was expected that inter-industry convergence around the information-intensive industry would be higher than any other pairs of convergence innovation. However, as expected, inter-industry convergence between the suppliers-dominated industry – which includes most traditional industries such as food processing (beverages, food stuffs, cigarettes, etc.), textiles, and metal products – and other industries showed the lowest degrees of convergence. They have been regarded as less innovative industries as well as technologically less adaptive to other industries. They may continue to have such characteristics.

4.3   *Convergence innovation matrix*

The degrees of inter-industry convergence can be expressed as a matrix form that is here called a convergence innovation matrix as seen in Table 6.2. Five rows and five columns represent five industrial types respectively. Each cell denotes the degree of convergence innovation among which shaded cells indicate intra-industry convergences and other cells indicate inter-industry convergences.

We can see that the greatest convergence appeared in inter-industry convergences between the scale-intensive industry and the science-based industry accounting for 48.9 percent of convergence patents out of total patents respectively. The highest degree of intra-industry convergence appeared within the

Table 6.2 Convergence innovation matrix by industrial types of Korea

	Sd	Ii	Ss	Si	Sb
Sd	8.26	7.59	11.03	10.70	11.05
Ii	7.59	25.40	28.73	26.05	21.66
Ss	11.03	28.73	45.27	44.61	41.29
Si	10.70	26.05	44.61	6.06	48.90
Sb	11.05	21.66	41.29	48.90	5.37

Notes: (1) unit of figures in each cell indicates percentage of convergence patents out of total patents, and (2) symbols of industrial types are the same as those described in Figure 6.5

specialized-suppliers industry revealing 45.3 percent of total US patents, followed by the information-intensive industry with 25.4 percent.

5.   Country differences in convergence innovation

5.1   *Cross-country comparison of patenting in the US*

A cross-country comparison of US patents applied for by Korea, Japan, Taiwan, and China offers an interesting insight into their innovation activities. While Japan is categorized as an advanced country, Korea and Taiwan are grouped into post catch-up countries, and China into a group of catching-up countries. Let us look at three industry types: the information-intensive industry, the specialized-suppliers industry, and the science-based industry. First, it is discovered that Japan is an absolute leader among four countries in US patenting in terms of scale in all three industrial sectors. However, the number of Japan's patent applications is somewhat decreasing, whereas that of Korea, Taiwan, and China is increasing. From the analysis of such trends, it is expected that the innovation gap between Japan and the other three countries will be narrowed down over the twelve years. In fact, export performance of Japanese industries has continuously declined, while that of the other three countries has improved during the same period.

The second interesting feature identified from the trends is that China caught up with the scale of US patenting activities of Taiwan both in the information-intensive industry and in the science-based industry as of 2008, and in the specialized-suppliers industry as of 2009. Chinese catch-up in all of the three industrial sectors implies that innovation capability and innovation performance of Chinese firms have already surpassed those of Taiwan. Chinese share in the export market has also exceeded that of Taiwan. It is surprising that Taiwan with relatively strong networks of small- and medium-sized firms tends to lose its innovation base in the specialized-suppliers industry, in which strong small- and medium-sized firms hold competitive advantage.

Lastly, Korea seems to have maintained the innovation gap with China while its gap with Japan in US patenting has been narrowed down up until 2012. Although some Korean industries have been losing their markets due to offensive entries of Chinese firms into global markets as explained in the case of the textile machinery industry in Chapter 7 of this book, overall patenting of the Korean industries in the United States – particularly three industrial types such as information intensive, specialized suppliers, and science based – has revealed an incremental trend as seen in (a), (b), and (c) respectively in Figure 6.6.

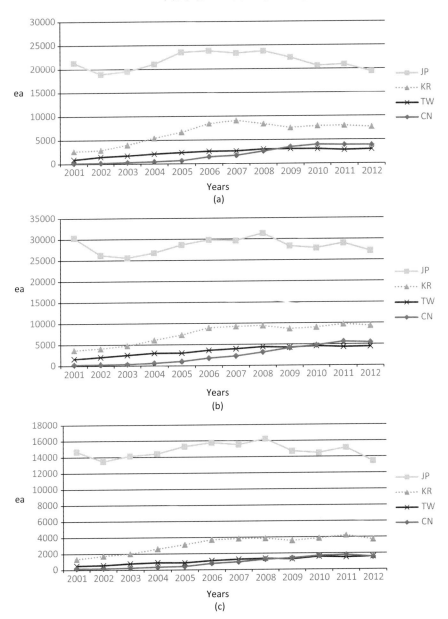

Figure 6.6 Country comparison of US patents in three industrial types: (a) information intensive, (b) specialized suppliers, and (c) science based

Notes: Abbreviations are as follows – JP denotes Japan, KR Korea, TW Taiwan, and CN China

These four countries have shown interesting dynamics in the innovation league of US patenting. The analysis of this inter-country dynamic reveals an overall decline of Japan's share and an anticipated increase in the shares of China and Korea over the coming decade. Therefore, innovation gaps among these four countries are expected to be narrowed down in the future. As the population size of the three countries except for Taiwan is substantially large, these three countries are likely to show a development pattern of one-set industry as a whole rather than specialization in some industrial sectors. This implies that sectoral differences in innovativeness in terms of US patenting among China, Japan, and Korea would be minimal.

5.2   Cross-country comparison of inter-industry convergence

Let us look at what happened in the convergence innovation in four countries. In order to compare the country differences in convergence innovation, we focused on the inter-industry convergence between the information-intensive and other three industrial types (Ss, Sd, Sb). Figure 6.7 reveals the trends of inter-industry convergence among the four countries. The degree of inter-industry convergence between the information-intensive and other three industrial types shows similar patterns by year. This similarity among four countries may be attributed to the fact that they have similar industrial structure and innovation culture.

The most striking difference appears in the inter-industry convergence between the information-intensive and the specialized suppliers. Against our expectations, the degree of the inter-industry convergence innovation (Ii-Ss) of China was the highest from 2001 to 2007 as seen in (a) of Figure 6.7. After 2007, Japan overtook China, but Korea remained in third place. However, the gaps among the four countries have been increasingly narrowed down as time goes by. It implies that the synchronization of the inter-industry convergence between the information-intensive and the specialized suppliers has been taking place across four countries affecting each other.

In terms of the inter-industry convergence between the information intensive and the suppliers dominated, Korea's average performance has been higher than other countries as shown in (b) of Figure 6.7. As seen from the convergence innovation matrix previously described, the lowest inter-industry convergence appeared in the pair of Ii-Sd (the information intensive and the supplier dominated) (7.59 percent). It is assumed that the supplier-dominated firms such as food processing, textile, metal product, glass, ceramics, and non-ferrous metal find it fundamentally difficult to take advantage of IT technologies through convergence innovation. Nonetheless, Korea shows a relatively high degree of convergence innovation compared to other countries as it had once strong suppliers-dominated industries like the textile industry.

Overall, there seems no major difference in the trends of inter-industry convergence by country. Rather, the inherent industrial and technological characteristics seem to play a critical role in convergence activities regardless of country-specific characteristics. Further investigation into cases of other countries is required to validate this argument.

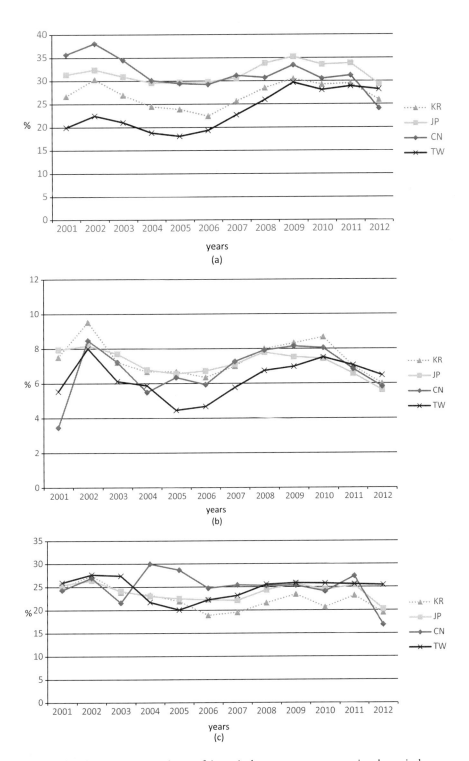

Figure 6.7 Country comparison of inter-industry convergences in three industry pairs: (a) Ii-Ss, (b) Ii-Sd, and (c) Ii-Sb

Notes: JP denotes Japan, KR Korea, CN China, and TW Taiwan

6.   Concluding remarks

We reviewed the trends and patterns of convergence innovation at both industry and country levels. Taking convergence characteristics that respond to the needs of different sources of innovation as well as the divergent market demands into account, diverse sources such as customers, ideas and knowledge of users and suppliers, knowledge-intensive services, scientific and technological knowledge, and networks can be triggers or drivers of convergence innovation. The ability to utilize such diverse sources strategically enables a firm to make convergence innovation and gain a unique advantage which becomes a core competence of the firm.

This chapter took a glimpse of the shape of convergence innovation both at sectoral and at country levels. It measured intra-industry convergence and inter-industry convergence and came up with a convergence innovation matrix based on the results of the analysis. The specialized-suppliers sector shows the highest degree of intra-convergence innovation accounting for 40 percent to 50 percent of total patents. It implies that the machinery industry has been rapidly innovating by integrating outside technologies. In terms of inter-industry convergence, the greatest inter-industry convergence appeared in the pair of Si-Sb (the scale intensive and the science based), followed by the convergence between the specialized suppliers and the scale intensive (Ss-Si), and between the specialized suppliers and the science based (Ss-Sb). This tendency implies that the machinery industry has been a focal point of convergence innovation integrating forward and backward industries.

The cross-country comparison of convergence innovation reveals an overall decline of Japanese and Taiwanese shares but increasing shares of China and Korea in the patenting in the US. These findings suggest that innovation gaps among these four countries be narrowed down in the future. We also found that there is no major difference in the trends of inter-industry convergence by country. Interestingly, a synchronization trend of the inter-industry convergence between the information-intensive and the specialized suppliers appears across four countries. It has been concluded from the cross-country comparison that the inherent industrial and technological characteristics may play a critical role in convergence activities regardless of country-specific characteristics.

This chapter adopted industry- and country-level approaches toward convergence innovation by quantitative measurement. As Gassmann and his colleagues (2010) argued, one needs to adopt nine different perspectives for exploiting future convergence innovations. The spatial perspective is concerned with globalization of convergence innovation – for instance, sourcing diverse knowledge by locating R&D centers in talented regions. The structural perspective deals with disaggregation of value chains of industries as one adopts greater specialization due to more complex technologies. The user perspective is to incorporate diverse user knowledge into the process of convergence innovation. The supplier perspective includes the downstream side of the innovation process like early integration of the suppliers' role. The leveraging perspective is to adopt business-model thinking, which is crucial in the commercialization of IPRs. The process perspective is to apply outside-in, inside-out, and coupled types of convergence innovation. The tool perspective is to adopt a set of instruments that enables customers to create or configure their own products. The institutional perspective deals with compensation, protection, co-exploitation of convergence innovation, and so on. Lastly, the cultural perspective is concerned with a mindset such as creation of community values and social norms, communication and trust between stakeholders, decision making of collective agents, and so on.

We hope that our findings will provide a clue to developing further theories on spatial, structure, process, institutional, and cultural aspects of convergence innovation. Innovation studies on convergence innovation need to deepen their framework toward various perspectives in the future. Research on convergence innovation with diverse angles will provide many useful insights into the exploration and exploitation of future innovation studies.

References

Fujimoto, T. (2007), "Architecture-based competitive advantage – a design information view of manufacturing", *Evolutionary and Institutional Economic Review*, vol. 4, no. 2, pp. 55–112.

Gassmann, O., Enkel, E. and Chesbrough, H. (2010), "The future of open innovation", *R&D Management*, vol. 40, no. 3, pp. 213–221.

Kodama, F. (1986), "Inter-disciplinary research: Japanese innovation in mechatronics technology", *Science and Public Policy*, vol. 13, no. 1, pp. 44–51.

Kodama, F. (1991), *Analyzing Japanese High Technologies: The Techno Paradigm Shift*, London: Pinter Publishers.

Kodama, F. (1994), *Emerging Patterns of Innovation*, Boston: Harvard University Press.

Lee, K.-R. (2007), "Patterns and processes of contemporary technology fusion: The case of intelligent robots", *Asian Journal of Technology Innovation*, vol. 15, no. 2, pp. 45–65.

Lee, K.-R. (2015), "Toward a new paradigm of technological innovation: Convergence innovation", *Asian Journal of Technology Innovation*, vol. 23, special issue, pp. 1–8.

Lee, K.-R. and Hwang, J.-T. (2005), *A Study on Innovation System with Multi-Technology Fusion* (in Korean), Seoul: STEPI Policy Study 2005–17.

Lee, K.-R. and Rhee, W. (2008), "Identifying leading industries and firms of Korea based on patent and export statistics", *Asian Journal of Technology Innovation*, vol. 16, no. 2, pp. 169–187.

Lee, K.-R., Yun, J.-H.J. and Jeong, E.-S. (2015), "Convergence innovation of the textile machinery industry in Korea", *Asian Journal of Technology Innovation*, vol. 23, special issue, pp. 58–73.

OECD (1993), *Technology Fusion: A Path to Innovation, the Case of Optoelectronics*, Paris: OECD.

Pavitt, K. (1984), "Sectoral patterns of technical change: Towards a taxonomy and a theory", *Research Policy*, vol. 13, no. 6, pp. 343–373.

Pavitt, K. (1992), "Paths: Exploiting technological trajectories", in *Managing Innovation*, pp. 169–202, London: Wiley.

Rosenberg, N. (1963), "Technological change in the machine tool industry, 1840–1910", *Journal of Economic History*, vol. 23, no. 4, pp. 414–446.

Rosenberg, N. (1982), *Inside the Black Box: Technology and Economics*, Cambridge: Cambridge University Press.

Tidd, J., Bessant, J. and Pavitt, K. (2001), *Managing Innovation*, Chichester: John Wiley & Sons.

7 Convergence innovation in specialized textile machinery suppliers in Korea

Kong-rae Lee

1. Introduction

Textile machinery is as diverse as the garments and clothes the textile industry manufactures. Manufacturing textile products requires various types of textile machinery and varying degrees of automation. Moreover, the emergence of information and telecommunication technology has made textile machinery a more complex system demanding diverse technological knowledge for innovation. Due to such circumstances, technological problems with textile machinery have been continuously shared and solved by different types of specialized textile machinery suppliers. Convergence innovation has necessarily prevailed among specialized textile machinery suppliers in modern times. It has evolved up to the point that other technologies are deeply integrated and even chemically mixed with textile machines.

Information and telecommunication suppliers and other related suppliers overall have a strong capability to support the innovation of textile machinery in Korea. With the assistance of various suppliers, textile production has been rapidly automated to offset the rising labor cost. As a result, Korean textile machinery suppliers have had opportunities to supply highly automated and innovated machines to their user firms by applying advanced IT technologies, possibly allowing specialized textile machinery suppliers to make convergence innovation. This has motivated the author to investigate specialized textile machinery suppliers of Korea.

This chapter aims to measure the degree of convergence innovation in the textile machinery industry and its trends among specialized textile machinery suppliers in Korea and to explore how convergence innovation takes place in the case of specialized textile machinery suppliers and what characteristics have emerged during their process of convergence innovation. There are two types of convergence innovation in textile machinery. One is the application of outside technologies to the innovation of textile machinery, which is called "outside-in convergence". The other is the application of textile machinery technology to the innovation of other machineries, which is termed "inside-out convergence". These two types of convergence innovation have been identified in the Korean textile machinery industry as the industry has suffered a considerable market loss incurred from the entries of the competing Chinese companies.

Section two of this chapter begins with the explanation of research methods to measure the degree of convergence innovation and data used in this study. In the third section, convergence innovation of specialized textile machinery suppliers is investigated in such detailed contents as processes and patterns of innovation, patenting activities of specialized suppliers in Korea, and measurement results of convergence. Section four introduces TnS as a case of an outside-in convergence innovator and Keumyong as a case of an inside-out convergence innovator. In the last section, concluding remarks are presented with some important implications.

2.   Research questions and methodology

The research methods of the present study have been chosen for the purpose of fulfilling the objectives of research. A key objective of the present study is to explore to what extent specialized textile machinery suppliers including their user firms and related suppliers have made convergence innovations in Korea. Other research questions include how convergence innovation takes place, what types of convergence emerge in the processes of innovation, and what are the characteristics of each convergence type in specialized textile machinery suppliers.

The research method adopted is an archival analysis mixed with field survey. The archival data used patent applications as a proxy for innovation. The US patent statistics have been used since they well represent the upstream part of the innovation cycle that includes various kinds of inventions like new ideas, prototypes, new processes, and designs. However, it does not well account for the degree of utilizations of certain innovation results such as software, trade secrets, and know-how associated with production processes. The time horizon of the data is twelve years, from 2001 to 2012.

As method to measure the degree of convergence innovation (CI), the percentage of patents with more than one USPTC class citation out of the total number of patents in each technology field has been calculated. It is assumed that the frequent occurrences of patents with more than one USPTC class citation indicate a high degree of convergence innovation. The degree of convergence innovation can be expressed as equation (1) where CP_{jt} indicates convergence patents with more than one USPTC class citation in textile machinery technology in innovator j at time period t. P_{jt} indicates the number of patent applications in textile machinery technology in innovator j at time period t. Convergence patents are defined as patents with more than one USPC class citation. CI_{jt} is a converted percentage index representing the degree of convergence innovation in textile machinery technology in innovator j at time period t.

$$CI_{jt} = \sum_{1}^{jt} \frac{CP_{jt}}{P_{jt}} \tag{1}$$

Together with the archival analysis, we adopted field surveys with CEOs of textile machinery companies to obtain their stories. Among interviewees are CEOs of specialized textile suppliers like Keumyong Co., TnS, and Ilsin Machine Co. and a CEO of a government-sponsored R&D institute, the Korea Textile Machinery Research Institute (KTMRI). KTMRI has played an important role in the Korean textile machinery industry as a liaison and coordinator in the Korean textile machinery innovation system. Their case stories are described in section four of this chapter.

3. Convergence innovation of specialized textile machinery suppliers

3.1 Processes of convergence innovation

Past innovation studies have explored cases of convergence innovation – for instance, case explorations on machine tools (Lee, 1998), intelligence robots (Lee, 2007; Lee and Hwang, 2005), printing technology (Lee and Seong, 2009), printed electronics (Kim, 2014), robotics (Kumaresan, 2001) and so on. Textile machine technology tends to be closely linked to textile technology through a typical process of convergence innovation. In fact, many international patent classifications (IPCs) associated with textile technologies are mixed with textile machine technologies, making it difficult to distinguish the two. We included mixed cases in textile machine technologies.

Euiseok Kim (2014) studied the convergence innovation between printing technology and electronic technology and argued that there is continuous disequilibrium between converging technologies which are divided into two kinds of technologies: reference technology and matching technology. These technologies tend to innovate at differing speeds in such a manner that when a reference technology is innovated generating disequilibrium, a matching technology necessarily innovates to match or adjust an optimal balance between the functions of the two technologies. He stated that the process of tuning through matching and minute adjustment between disparate technologies to achieve a target performance is one of the most critical attributes in convergence innovation.

Textile machinery tends to show a convergence process depicted in Figure 7.1. As time goes by a textile machine supplier learns new technological knowledge (T_{a1}) at time period t_0, and develops a new machine (T_{a2}) by converging a matching technology (T_{b2}). It is an innovation at time period of t_1, which may be incremental or radical. At time t_2, textile machinery suppliers or user firms again integrate new technological knowledge (T_{b2}) as technology (T_{a2}) at time t_1 becomes obsolete. The outcome of this process is new functions or new products created by textile machinery suppliers or their user firms through the convergence like that of time t_1. This process repeatedly takes place until time t_n unless they stop the learning process.

It may be, however, much more complex in reality than this simplified process. In that sense, both reference technology and integrated technology may have a certain degree of capability in the process of convergence or adjusting an optimal balance. This capability may imply a technological opportunity to innovate individual technologies so as to converge the two technologies involved and ultimately make a convergence innovation.

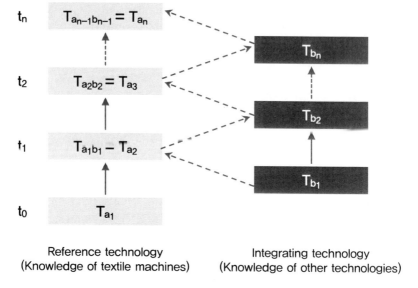

Reference technology
(Knowledge of textile machines)

Integrating technology
(Knowledge of other technologies)

Figure 7.1 A process of convergence innovation

As such, the processes of convergence innovation can be found in many innovation cases not only in the metal processing machines of the twentieth century as explored by Rosenberg (1963, 1982) but also in the current times. It is also perceived that such processes of convergence innovation can be universally applied to all technological fields and industrial areas (OECD, 1993; Rafols and Meyer, 2006; Roco and Bainbridge, 2002). The innovation of textile machinery seems to have typical characteristics of convergence similar to that of machine tools, intelligence robots, printed electronics, robotics, and so forth.

This conjecture is based upon the IPCs (international patent codes) structure of textile machinery patents. Textile machinery patents with two IPCs recorded 5,821 in numbers accounting for 32.7 percent of the total patents during the period of 2000–2011. In same way, it was discovered that textile machinery patents with three IPCs were 4,451 (25.1 percent), and those with four IPCs were 3,071 (17.3 percent). As a result, textile machinery patents with more than two IPCs indicating convergence innovation accounted for 50.1 percent of the total patents during the same period (Lee, Yun and Jeong, 2015).

3.2   *Textile machinery innovation in Korea*

Table 7.1 explains the trend of shares of textile machinery patents by three types of textile machinery innovators: related suppliers, textile firms or user firms, and specialized textile machinery suppliers. By 2004, related suppliers dominated patenting in textile machinery as they accounted for 85.7 percent in 2004 though they declined afterwards. The declining trend of the related suppliers after 2004 was due to the recession of the textile machinery industry. Domestic textile machinery suppliers suffered from the entries of the Chinese textile machinery suppliers with cheap prices into the global market since 2004. Many Korean suppliers exited textile machinery markets, resulting in a rapid contraction of the industry size.

The share of textile machinery patents adopted by textile firms who are users of textile machinery had decreased until 2004. It, however, jumped back quickly from 13.4 percent in 2005 to 35.0 percent in 2011 as seen in Table 7.1. The increasing share of user firms in textile machinery patents seems desirable because active engagement of user firms in the innovation of textile machinery will ultimately lead to competence building of the textile machinery industry (Lee, 1998). CEOs of Korean textile firms do not seem to know how to make convergence innovation that requires diverse knowledge and technologies. To reduce cost, they

Table 7.1 Patenting trends in textile machinery by types of firms in Korea

Classification	2000–2003	2004–2007	2008–2011	Total (%)
National total (A)	5,186	7,752	7,888	20,826 (100.0)
User firms (C)	2,175	3,405	4,419	9,999 (48.0)
Users: textile firms (C1)	66	192	1,682	1,940 (9.3)
Other users (individuals) (C2)	2,109	3,213	2,737	8,059 (38.7)
Specialized textile machine suppliers (D)	66	192	440	698 (3.4)
Other related suppliers (R)	2,945	4,155	3,029	10,129 (48.6)
Electronics	2,159	3,333	1,909	7,401 (35.5)
Chemical	331	351	410	1,092 (5.2)
Metal products	125	183	194	502 (2.4)
Electrical appliances	206	5	26	237 (1.1)
Paper products	23	67	92	182 (0.9)
Motors	13	43	92	148 (0.7)
Machinery industry	29	79	125	233 (1.1)
Construction	9	30	67	106 (0.5)
Materials	16	25	52	93 (0.4)
Food, medical and pharmaceutical	17	24	36	77 (0.3)
Others	17	15	26	58 (0.3)
Ratio of user firms (C/A)	41.9	43.9	56.0	48.0
Ratio of specialized suppliers (D/A)	1.3	2.5	5.6	3.4
Ratio of related suppliers ([D+R]/A)	58.1	56.1	44.0	52.0

Source: Lee et al. (2015); Website of Korean Intellectual Property Rights Information Service: http//kipris.or.kr

rather sought to exit from the textile business or invest in less-developed countries with cheaper labor cost instead of innovating production processes by integrating capital goods technologies.

Although many textile firms have exited from the textile industry, technological problems on textile machinery seemed to be continuously shared and solved by different types of specialized textile machinery suppliers. Statistics on textile machinery patents implies that convergence innovation has prevailed in the innovation of textile machinery for instance. As has been the case of other technology fields, electronics technology which accounts for the largest share in the total patents (35.5 percent) has been integrated into textile machinery by specialized suppliers. Other technologies have also been integrated into textile machinery, but not much, as shown in Table 7.1. It has evolved up to the point that other technologies are deeply integrated into and even chemically mixed with textile machines, resulting in completely new types of textile machinery.

Processing chemical fibers require a complex machinery system that is often called a plant. Making cloths and garments by using material fibers requires various weaving machines. The innovations of weaving machines need not only mechanical technology but also some textile technologies. Thus, user firms have room to contribute to the innovation of new weaving machines. Engineers from specialized suppliers often stay at customer factories for an extended period. If they identify problems with the new machinery, they report them to their own companies and carry out additional R&D work to solve the identified problems and thus improve the new machines (Sugiura, 1994). New textile machines are therefore completed by suppliers and users who exchange and integrate their expertise through frequent interactions. We can identify such innovation taking place in textile machinery as convergence innovation.

It has been generally accepted among innovation studies that user firms play important roles in the innovation of specialized suppliers. It is the user who generates ideas for a new product and makes, evaluates and implements an in-house prototype, particularly in such capital goods as machine tools, scientific instruments and others (Lee, 1998; von Hippel, 1988). A study on a Korean case reported that the important sources of technological innovation are customers (35.0 percent), followed by competing firms (20.0 percent), machinery suppliers (14.2 percent), part suppliers (13.9 percent), universities (12.3 percent) and others (Lee and Seong, 2009).

In Korea, the number of textile firms that have played the role of lead users seems to be limited. They may have not known that there are large-scale textile markets – for example, medical textiles for the medical service sector and industrial textiles for the automotive industry. Only a few firms took the risk of entering into high value added textile markets because it requires burdensome investment in R&D. As result, specialized textile machine suppliers had to suffer from decreased domestic demand and less pressure for the development of new textile machinery, which further contracted the real demand for domestic textile machines. Consequently, many specialized suppliers lying at a marginal profit line had to exit the textile machinery business.

Innovations made by specialized textile machinery suppliers are not impressive compared with those of user firms. The top ten patenting specialized suppliers are listed in Table 7.2. The first is Sunster Co. with eighty-seven patents, followed by Sunstar Precision Co. with sixty-nine patents. The third is the Korea Textile Machinery Research Institute (KTMRI) with twenty-eight patents, followed by Inbro Co. (fourth with twenty-six applications), Sunstar R&C Co. (fifth with fourteen), Dae Hung Hitech Co. (sixth with fourteen), Daelim Starlet Co. (seventh with ten), Ilsung Machine Industry Co. (eighth with nine), Ssangyong Machinery Co. (ninth with nine), and lastly Dae Kwang Co. (tenth with six). Two affiliate companies of Sunstar appeared to be the most innovative specialized textile machinery suppliers in Korea. Interestingly, KTMRI and Dyetec Center, both government-sponsored research institutes, took the leading positions in patenting activities. Ssangyong Machinery Co. was once a well-known specialized textile machinery supplier, but it has recently lost its drive in innovation.

In summary, R&D work not only for the innovation of textiles but also for the innovation of new textile machines has been lacking in Korea over the last decade. It was already pointed out as an issue in a policy study in the 1980s (Ha, 1987). Even after decades have passed, either user firms or specialized suppliers do not invest much resources into R&D activities nor integrate market characteristics into R&D activities as suggested by the fourth-generation R&D. They could not succeed in recruiting good researchers and electronics engineers who supplement their development work. They did not take R&D work into account seriously during the time when Chinese suppliers accumulated the capability to manufacture cheap textile machines and dominated the global textile machinery market. Convergence innovation of specialized suppliers might well be minimal as user-supplier interactions reduced and learning opportunities dwindled.

Table 7.2 Top 10 patenting specialized textile machinery suppliers in Korea

Ranks	Name of firms	'00–'03	'04–'07	'08–'11	Total
1	Sunstar Co. Ltd.	11	43	33	87
2	Sunstar Precision Co.	30	31	8	69
3	KTMRI	0	6	22	28
4	Inbro Co. Ltd	12	14	0	26
5	Sunstar R&C Co., Ltd.	0	0	14	14
6	Dae Hung Hitech Co., Ltd.	4	2	6	12
7	Daelim Starlet Co., Ltd.	3	3	4	10
8	Ilsung Machine Industry Co., Ltd.	3	1	5	9
9	Ssangyong Machinery Co., Ltd.	5	3	1	9
10	Dae Kwang Co., Ltd.	0	0	6	6

Source: Lee et al. (2015)

3.3　*Degree of convergence innovation*

To what degree has convergence innovation been carried out in the textile machinery industry in Korea? An analysis of US textile machinery patents has been made using the methods described in section two. From the analysis, it was found out that the degree of convergence innovation in textile machinery has continuously increased during the period of 2001–2011 as shown in Figure 7.2. In 2001, the ratio of convergence innovation in the total patents was only 1.9 percent, which jumped to 62.8 percent in 2011. That means 1,203 US patents appeared to be convergence patents with more than two IPCs out of a total 1,915 US patents in 2011. This trend reveals a steady increase of convergence innovation, perhaps predominant in textile machinery innovation.

It is interesting to see why the innovation of textile machinery showed such convergence features. It may be because textile machinery is as diverse as the garments or clothes the textile industry produces. Manufacturing different kinds of textile products requires different kinds of textile machinery and varying degrees of automation depending on the wage level in the manufacturing countries. Moreover, the emergence of information and telecommunication technology has made textile machinery more complex, demanding diverse technological knowledge for innovation. Convergence innovation of specialized textile machinery suppliers has necessarily prevailed in modern times.

It was also discovered that the degree of convergence innovation varies by types of innovators. Specialized suppliers showed the highest ratio of convergence

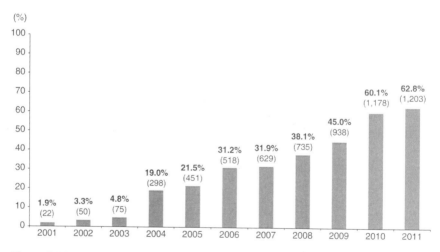

Figure 7.2 Trends of convergence innovation (CI) ratios in the textile machinery industry of Korea

Note: Figures in parentheses are the number of convergence patents

Source: Websites of the Korea Intellectual Property Rights Information Service (kipris.or.kr) and the Korean Statistical Information Service (kosis.kr)

innovation in their total innovations, 80.9 percent for the period of 2000–2011, followed by user firms with 70.2 percent. Other related suppliers that are not specialized in the production of textile machinery showed 43.6 percent on average for the same period. Among those related suppliers, motor manufacturers and construction firms showed the highest ratio of convergence innovation as seen in Figure 7.3. Electronics suppliers were expected to show a high degree of convergence innovation, but their ratio remained at only 37.0 percent. Electrical appliances suppliers showed the lowest degree of convergence innovation, as their ratio recorded only 11.8 percent.

In order to review convergence innovation of the textile machinery industry in detail, ten key component technologies have been identified from a whole range of IPCs in the textile machinery industry for making a matrix comparison. Component technologies affecting the convergence innovation of specialized suppliers were grouped into two types. One is user sources that include such knowledge about fibers as super fibers, high performance fibers, industrial material fibers, high functional fibers, and cloth and life material fibers. This knowledge is basically embedded in the experts of user firms – in other words, textile firms. The other is such sources related to mechanical technology as basic mechanical engineering, material technologies, conventional machining, automation, control technologies and IT technologies. They are obviously embedded in the experts of specialized suppliers or other related suppliers from various industries (Lee et al., 2015).

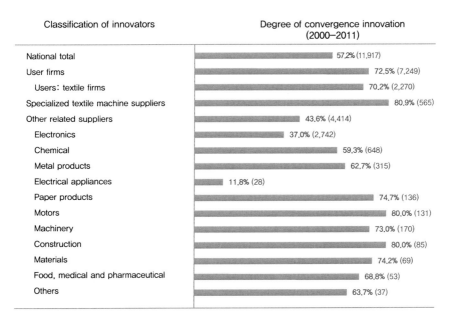

Figure 7.3 Degrees of convergence innovation (CI) by types of innovators

Note: Figures in parentheses are the number of convergence patents.

Through the analysis, eight key component technologies based on IPCs have been chosen, which are presumably related to more than one thousand patents. They are D06F (laundering technologies), D01F (fibers technology), D06M (treatment technology), D21H (pulp composition), D04B (knitting), D01D (mechanical methods), D03D (weaving) and D05B (sewing). With eight component technologies, a convergence innovation matrix of textile machinery technology was constructed as seen in Table 7.3.

The convergence innovation matrix tells us component technologies that are frequently converging. It indicates, however, convergence innovation took place within textile machinery clusters. Component technologies included in the matrix are highly possible to be reference technology that is converged or matching technology that is converging. As shown in Table 7.3, frequent convergences took place between D01D (mechanical methods) and D01F (fibers technology) with 619 patents, between D03D (weaving) and D06M (treatment technology) with 158 patents, between D06M (treatment technology) and D01F (fibers technology) with 114 patents, and between D03D (weaving) and D01F (fibers technology) with 100 patents. At the four digit level of IPCs, we can see that mechanical methods, fiber technology and weaving technology are key components of convergence innovation in textile machinery. Mechanical methods may represent many input technologies applied to convergence innovation. For instance, electronics technology may be included in D01D (mechanical methods) and may have been greatly applied to convergence innovation of textile machinery.

Table 7.3 Convergence innovation matrix of textile machinery technologies

	D06F	D01F	D06M	D21H	D04B	D01D	D03D	D05B
D06F	8,484							
D01F		2,268	114	15	24	619	100	
D06M		114	2,049	14	31	47	158	3
D21H		15	14	1,729		5	2	
D04B		24	31		1,315	10	66	6
D01D		629	47	5	10	1,131	28	
D03D		100	158	2	66	28	1,096	5
D05B			3		6		5	1,078

Notes: D06F (technology related to laundering, drying, ironing, pressing or folding textile articles), D01F (chemical features in the manufacture of artificial filaments, threads, fibers, bristles or ribbons, apparatus specially adapted for the manufacture of carbon filaments), D06M (treatment technology of threads, yarns, fabrics or fibrous goods by chemical, biochemical or physical means), D06M (treatment, not provided for elsewhere in class D06, of fibers, threads, yarns, fabrics, feathers or fibrous goods made from such materials), D21H (pulp compositions), D04B (knitting), D01D (mechanical methods or apparatus in the manufacture of artificial filaments, threads, fibers, bristles or ribbons), D03D (woven fabrics, methods of weaving, looms) and D05B (sewing technology)

4. Two types of convergence innovation in textile machinery suppliers

4.1 Outside-in convergence: case of TnS

From the interviews with specialized suppliers, it has been implied that convergence innovation of textile machinery has been taking place in two ways. One is the application of other technologies to the innovation of textile machinery as depicted in Figure 7.4 (a), in which C_1, C_2, . . . and C_5 indicate core technologies of a firm and T_1, T_2 and T_3 stand for outside technologies of the firm. A_1 and A_2 indicate current textile machines of the firm before convergence while A_{11} and A_{21} stand for new machines manufactured after converging outside technologies. Figure 7.4 (a) shows how outside-in convergence innovation takes place in a firm.

Outside-in convergence is mostly found in specialized textile machinery suppliers. It is likely to be active when the textile machinery industry is in a booming period because the increasing demand for textile machinery leads to an

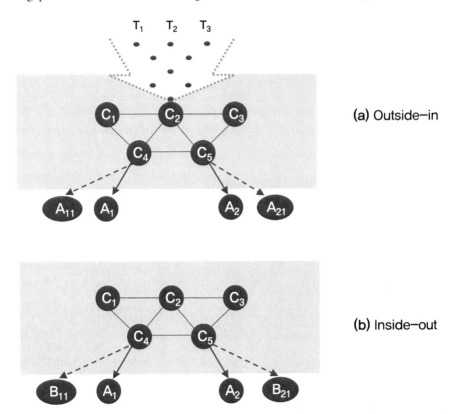

(a) Outside–in

(b) Inside–out

Figure 7.4 Two types of convergence innovation in textile machinery innovators

increase in its output and technical problems, which in turn generate more innovations to solve them along with innovation of related suppliers. The most frequently integrated outside technologies for the innovation of textile machinery appeared to be electronic control technology and information and communication technology. Such outside technologies were integrated into new textile machines such as digital textile printing (DTP), automatic sewing thread winders, water jet and air jet rapier looms, knitting machines and others. Integration was made possible through R&D work of specialized suppliers or by simply combining embedded parts and components manufactured by other related suppliers. Examples of this outside-in convergence are found in TnS and Ilsin Machine Co., who are specialized textile machinery suppliers, and in the Korea Textile Machinery Research Institute (KTMRI), a government sponsored research center.

TnS among these firms provides an interesting story about outside-in convergence innovation. Mr. Song Jae-sung, president of the firm, has been specialized in the integration of electronic and computer technologies into various textile machines for more than twenty years. He has manufactured such automation systems as EZ-cords, single raschel EL controller, double raschel EL controller, piezo jacquard for warp knitting machine (Figure 7.5), and jacquardless system. He has been successful in making these textile machines read a database containing professional designers' graphic designs and weave textiles according to the computerized designs. The company has also integrated computer and control technologies into various textile machines under operation so as to contribute to their process innovations. The convergence effort of TnS has turned old textile machines into automatic and smart machines. As result, textile firms have been able to substantially increase productivity by adopting such computerized machines.

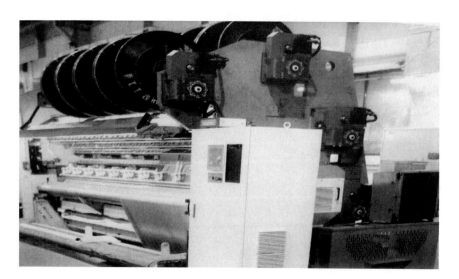

Figure 7.5 A high-speed warp knitting machine innovated by KnS

4.2   Inside-out convergence: case of Keumyong

The second type of convergence innovation is the application of textile machinery technology to the innovation of other machinery. This type of innovation is called inside-out convergence innovation as seen in Figure 7.4 (b), in which C_1, C_2 and C_5 indicate core technologies of a firm. A_1 and A_2 indicate current textile machines of the firm before convergence, while B_{11} and B_{21} stand for new machines manufactured after converging the existing core technologies of the firm. The firm does not utilize outside technologies, but instead integrates its core technologies that exist inside of the firm for convergence innovation. The process of inside-out convergence may be explained with the concept proposed by Nonaka (1994), the "externalization" of internal knowledge. This firm may, in other words, not be interested in open innovation, whereas firms carrying out outside-in convergence innovation may feel interested.

Inside-out convergence innovation has been also taking place in specialized suppliers, but it has not been frequent because specialized suppliers do not attempt completely new businesses as they tended to develop new items based on their core competence accumulated from textile machinery business. This type of convergence was discovered in the Korean textile machinery industry as it has suffered a market loss incurred from the entries of Chinese companies. Inside-out convergence is likely to be active during the recession period because specialized suppliers seek to maintain employees and operate existing production facilities by entering into technologically possible markets.

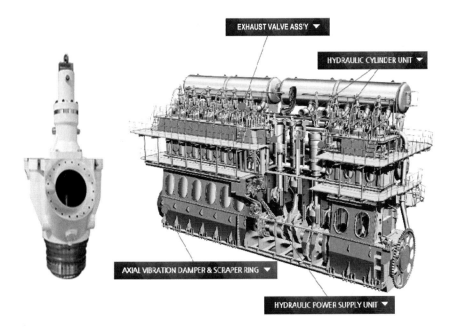

Figure 7.6 An exhaust valve and ship engine made by Keumyong

Keumyong Co. has specialized in the manufacturing of knitting machines such as jersey knitting machines, stripper machines, computerized jacquard machines, seamless machines and so on. The company tried to find application areas by utilizing its circular ring processing technology regarded as its core competence when the domestic market for textile machinery was seriously shrinking. Based on technological capability in circular ring processing, the company developed exhaust valves of a ship engine as seen in Figure 7.6 and successfully attracted buyers in the domestic market. As a result of the company's doing business in exhaust valves for many years, now more than half of its sales come from exhaust valves. Keumyong's core business has now changed from textile machinery to ship engine valves. Inside-out convergence was a way of exiting the textile machinery industry under severe recession and entering into a new booming industry as described previously.

5. Concluding remarks

From the analysis of US patenting activities of the Korean textile machinery companies, we obtained some findings with respect to convergence innovation. Overall, the innovation of both textile firms and specialized textile machinery suppliers was weak compared with that of other machinery industries in Korea. Weak innovation performance has been mainly due to the sluggish R&D activities of textile machinery suppliers. This chapter investigated convergence innovation of specialized suppliers and found some meaningful results.

First, the degree of convergence innovation in textile machinery suppliers has continuously increased over the period of 2001–2011. The ratio of convergence innovation was merely 1.9 percent of the total patents in 2001, but it jumped to 62.8 percent in 2011 in ten years. This trend reveals that convergence innovation has steadily increased, and it has now become a dominant phenomenon in the technological innovation of the textile machinery industry. This indicates that the contemporary manufacturing industry is now taking a new paradigm of convergence innovation.

Second, the degree of convergence innovation varies by types of innovators. Specialized textile machinery suppliers showed the highest ratio of convergence innovation out of total innovations, accounting for 80.9 percent during the period of 2000–2011, followed by user firms with 70.2 percent. Other related suppliers that are not specialized in the production of textile machinery showed 43.6 percent on average for the same period. With the viewpoint of component technologies, the most distinctive convergence within textile machinery technologies has been taking place between mechanical methods (D01D) and fibers technology (D01F). These two technologies are representative components of textile and textile machinery technology respectively.

Third, two types of convergence innovation have been identified in textile machinery: outside-in convergence and inside-out. Inside-out convergence is an innovation that integrates textile machinery technology into other technology areas, and outside-in convergence is vice versa. The former is likely to be active in current textile machinery suppliers who are utilizing their core competence for exploiting business opportunities in other machines as the case of Keumyong. They are now struggling to survive in the market recession and over-supply from Chinese competitors with cheaper prices. On the other hand, outside-in convergence innovations were also discovered in specialized suppliers like TnS. The most frequently integrated outside technologies appeared to be electronic control and information and communication technologies.

In conclusion, convergence innovation of specialized textile machinery suppliers becomes more and more important for their competence building as their user firms increasingly demand complex machinery and systems in order to increase their productivity. Korean specialized suppliers have responded to this technological environment as they continued to increase convergence innovation. Some specialized suppliers like TnS and Keumyong seem to have been successful in carrying out two types of convergence innovation respectively. They are likely to remain competitive as long as they continue to carry out convergence innovation. Although this chapter deals with only one industry case, it provides important implications for policy and management strategy of other manufacturing firms. Certainly further case investigations into different industries will offer more fruitful results.

References

Ha, J.-Y. (1987), *Technology Development System and Market Structure of the Korean Textile Machinery Industry* (in Korean), Seoul: KIET Research Report.

Kim, E. (2014), *Evolutionary Patterns and Dynamics of Technological Convergence: The Case of Printed Electronics*, PhD Dissertation, Daejeon: KAIST.

Kumaresan, N. (2001), *Dynamics of Technology Accumulation and Evolution of Distributed Industries: The Case of Robotics Industry*, Ph.D. Thesis, Tokyo: Tokyo Institute of Technology.

Lee, K.-R. (1998), *The Sources of Capital Goods Innovation: The Roles of User Firms in Japan and Korea*, London: Harwood Academic Publishers.

Lee, K.-R. (2007), "Patterns and processes of contemporary technology fusion: The case of intelligent robots", *Asian Journal of Technology Innovation*, vol. 15, no. 2, pp. 45–65.

Lee, K.-R. and Hwang, J.-T. (2005), *A Study on Innovation System with Multi-Technology Fusion* (in Korean), Seoul: STEPI Policy Study 2005–17.

Lee, K.-R. and Seong, T.-G. (2009), *University-Industry Collaboration for Activating Convergence Innovation* (in Korean), Seoul: STEPI Policy Report.

Lee, K.-R., Yun, J. J. and Jeong, E.-S. (2015), "Convergence innovation of the textile machinery industry in Korea", *Asian Journal of Technology Innovation*, vol. 23, no. s.1, pp. 58–73.

Nonaka, I. (1994), "A dynamic theory of organizational knowledge creation", *Organizational Science*, vol. 5, no. 1, pp. 14–37.

OECD (1993), *Technology Fusion: A Path to Innovation, the Case of Optoelectronics*, Paris: OECD.

Rafols, I. and Meyer, M. (2006), *Knowledge-Sourcing Strategies for Cross-Disciplinarity in Bionanotechnology*, Brighton: SPRU Electronic Working Paper Series, no. 152.

Roco, M. C. and Bainbridge, W. S. (2002), *Converging Technologies for Improving Human Performance*, Arlington, VA: NSF.

Rosenberg, N. (1963), "Technological change in the machine tool industry, 1840–1910", *Journal of Economic History*, vol. 23, no. 4, pp. 414–446.

Rosenberg, N. (1982), *Inside the Black Box: Technology and Economics*, Cambridge: Cambridge University Press.

Sugiura, K. (1994), *Technological Role of Machinery Users in Economic Development: The Case of the Textile Machinery Industry in Japan and Korea*, PhD Dissertation, Brighton: University of Sussex.

von Hippel, E. (1988), *The Source of Innovation*, New York: Oxford University Press.

Website of Korean Statistical Information Service: http//kosis.kr.

8 Convergence innovation in city innovation system

Railway technology case in Malaysia

Chan-Yuan Wong

1. Introduction

The life cycle of product development and process innovation has been the subject of research among innovation scholars and industrial policymakers. The intellectual discussion – as it appears in scientific publications – is deemed valuable towards understanding the structure of an innovation system at the sectoral level. An understanding of such structures is useful for policymakers in planning and executing both targeted and functional technological catching-up strategies for industrial development. Many catching-up case studies that explained the perspective of product development and process innovation life cycles have provided insights, policy guides and implications for economies aspiring to emulate the path of upgrading and development (e.g. Kim, 1997, Malerba and Mani, 2009, Mathews and Cho, 2000, Teubal and Andersen, 2000, Vona and Consoli, 2014).

While the theoretical perspective of life cycles has been useful for narrating a technological and economic development process, it also inspires scholars to explore the convergence processes of different industries and technologies. A process is often regarded as change where different technologies emerge at the intersection of defined industry boundaries (Karvonen and Kassi, 2013). The change can be stimulated via the interstices of information and communication technologies (ICT) or material science and technology (Hacklin, Martx and Fahni, 2009, Lee, 2015 and Steinmueller, 2014). The interstices can be used as a complementary platform for the agents of change to perform combination and recombination of different technologies.

There are many scholars who advocate the capital city as the space for the convergence process (Tang, 2015, Thiruchelvam, Hassan and Daud, 2014 and Yusuf and Nabeshima, 2005). A country's capital city is a space where labor market pooling and sharing as well as technological spillovers can be found (Clare, 2013, Rimmer and Dick, 2009 and Yusuf and Nabeshima, 2005). It provides local and international enterprises with an efficient location for:

1   Markets for skilled or talented labor, professionals and managers;
2   Frequent national and international transport connections (thus providing the most accessible information and searching costs); and

3   A sizable segment of affluent consumers who are likely to create consumer value for firms.

Tokyo, for example, witnessed the co-existence of high-tech manufacturing activities, various value-added services for manufacturing industries, and the creative industries. The existence of different industries created a complementary environment that led Tokyo to gain a competitive advantage in performing convergence innovation. The environment attracted talent pools to perform various tasks, including research and design for high-tech production; creating prototypes or manufacturing initial batches of new products; and then using the local market as a test bed to examine the market response to the new products. Such synergy attracted talent from various backgrounds, such as those with tacit knowledge on production; experts (e.g. from universities and public research institutes [PRIs]) who are competent in performing basic and applied research; those with the ability to integrate different technologies and knowledge for specific tasks; and those skilled in advertising, marketing and distributing new products in the city. It is argued that such synergy induced different entities in the city to cooperate for convergence innovation and maintained costly activities and growth (Yusuf and Nabeshima, 2005).

This implies that non-capital cities within the country are likely to impose higher overall unit costs and place firms at a competitive disadvantage (Rimmer and Dick, 2009, p. 93). Many successful creative enterprises emerged from capital cities that provided conditions for a convergence innovation process. The industrial agglomeration or city innovation system – occasioned by the interactive environment and frequent technological spillover events in the city space – is seen to propel the convergence prospects for technological innovation (Markatou and Alexandrou, 2015 and Thiruchelvam et al., 2014).

Many East Asian economies witnessed the growth of high-tech innovative activities in producer services and the creative industries, clustered within their globally linked capital cities. The activities led to enormous growth in their respective economies. Scholars observe that high-tech related industries – such as R&D, software production and design – are commonly found in the capital cities in Asia. This observation corresponds to the significant size of these industries (52 percent) compared to the entirety of the creative industries (including media, art and culture) globally. The significant growth of these industries in East Asian capital cities is evident in Yusuf and Nabeshima (2005).

Reading from the literature informs us that there are basically two major types of local business ownership in the city space, which are:

1   Conglomerate firms that diversify in backward type of investments (e.g. the supply of construction materials and services) and forward type of investments (e.g. finance, utilities, telecommunications, retailing, transport, health care and education) (Rimmer and Dick, 2009, pp. 196–226). Many firms used to capitalize on factor accumulation and relied on banking and financial activities to expand their businesses to the international market. The structural change of East Asia (focusing on high-tech and high-value-added

industries) has influenced them to compete for dominant positions in networks and ICT infrastructure building. These firms are able to mobilize huge sums of resources and thus are capable of constructing urban network infrastructures (e.g. rail, road, water, power, gas, telecommunications, etc.).

2   City dwellers, urbanites or individuals who have the ability to perform high-value added activities. They ventured into both small- (e.g. SMEs) and large-scale manufacturing businesses. They also can provide niche services that address specific problems and create software to support the control systems of the larger organizations (Vona and Consoli, 2014). Those who could perform in these highly organized businesses attained a sophisticated level of skills. Venture capital firms were established to provide them with funding and other supports to venture into niche businesses. Universities and public research institutions are endowed with resources to support those entrepreneurs who wish to venture into high-tech startups (Intarakumnerd, 2011, Wong, 2011, and Wong, Hu and Shiu, 2015). The endowments are also used to induce and furnish an urban environment (via various incubation centers) that supports startups, which in turn leads to the rapid growth of the economy.

As a typical industrializing economy in the race to acquire niche positions in the global technological value chain, Malaysia launched and executed various programs in order to attain an economic structure based on knowledge and innovation-oriented production. Thus, exploring the knowledge clusters of the major industrial agglomerations in Malaysia would provide us with insights into how convergence innovations can take place in the pursuit of acquiring the desired economic structure. Following the pioneering work of agglomeration and writing on city innovation systems, this chapter attempts to explore the knowledge landscapes of Kuala Lumpur and its adjoining science and industrial park, Cyberjaya, in their production of information and communication services in the state of Selangor. This would allow us to explore the evolving knowledge structure of Kuala Lumpur that has been observed to have contributed substantially (34 percent) to national GDP (Rimmer and Dick, 2009, see p. 91).

By studying the density of patenting activities and intensity of knowledge ties developed to fuse new industries, this chapter seeks to highlight the knowledge clusters in Kuala Lumpur that shaped the path of convergence innovation. This chapter provides a case study on railway technology in order to understand why Express Rail Link Sdn Bhd (ERL) was determined to invest in convergence innovation for rail services, and what rail technology emerged in the pursuit of both technological and business expansions.

2.   Research methodology

2.1   *Conceptual guide*

This chapter draws on substantial materials and literature, which describe a functional regional system for innovation and elaborate on the notion of convergence innovation (Autio, 1998, Bresnahan, Gambardella and Saxenian, 2005,

Cooke, Uranga and Etxebarria, 1997, Foray, 2006, Porter, 1998, Potter, Whittington and Powell, 2005, Sorenson, 2005, Su and Wu, 2015, and Wong, Chandran and Ng, 2014). These works draw from the perspective of economics, industrial dynamics and organizational learning by searching. This study recognizes the importance of the industrial cluster, as it reflects the density of firms in an industrial agglomeration and is a method by which the firms form alliances to secure a niche position in the global value chain. This study acknowledges the complementary knowledge assets that configured the structure of a city innovation system. The perspective of Markusen (1996) on hub-and-spoke districts (see Table 8.1) provided us with a guide in narrating the knowledge cluster of Kuala Lumpur. The mentioned features indeed resemble the dynamic agglomeration aspect that can be observed in Kuala Lumpur. The city concentrates on its niche as a commodities exchange, where a number of key firms (e.g. Petronas and Shell) and infrastructures (e.g. telecommunication and transport hubs) that are capable of meeting specific needs of multinationals (MNCs) emerged as anchors to the regional economy (Rimmer and Dick, 2009, p. 79). The established infrastructures are intended to attract global control functions and producer services that support multinational operations. To this existing literature, this analysis will add our observations on knowledge clusters and ties that led to the fusion of new industries.

2.2 Data and methods

Many studies in the literature have found patent statistics useful or even instrumental in gaining hindsight and understanding on various innovation subjects and patterns. These include studies on scientific and technological trajectory (e.g. Schmoch, 2007), innovation system performance (e.g. Nesta and Patel,

Table 8.1 Selected features of a hub-and-spoke district

- Business structure dominated by several large, vertically integrated firms that are surrounded by suppliers
- Long-term contracts and commitments between dominant firms and suppliers
- High degrees of cooperation, linkages with external firms – both locally and externally
- Workers committed to large firms
- Specialized sources of finance, technical expertise, business services – dominated by large firms
- Strong local government role in regulating and promoting core industries
- High degree of public involvement in providing infrastructure
- Long-term prospects for growth dependent upon prospects for the industry and strategies of dominant firms
- Substantial intra-district trade among dominant firms and suppliers
- Relatively high economy of scale

Source: Markusen (1996, p. 298)

2004 and Wong and Goh, 2012), co-evolution between science, technology and development (e.g. Bernadas and Albuquerque, 2003 and Fagerberg, Srholec and Knell, 2007), impact of funded R&D (e.g. Wang and Hagedoorn, 2014), networks and linkages (e.g. Potter, Whittington and Powell, 2005), economic and technological catching-up (e.g. Lee, 2013 and Odagiri, Goto and Nelson, 2010) and management of innovation (e.g. Islam and Ozcan, 2015). They find that patent statistics can provide valuable information that allows them to explore the knowledge on innovation via an inductive approach. The statistics also provide them with a tool to validate their theoretical perspective, via corroborating the patenting pattern with the proposed narrative on innovation processes. Some capitalize on both patenting data and econometrics modeling to provide a rigorous mathematical model, which is useful for forecasting tasks. Patents have become the common proxy for technological innovation in many studies (Grupp, 1996, 1998 and Jaffe and Trajtenberg, 2002). They can provide reflections on (but are not limited to):

1   Technology progress, via exploring the patent portfolio;
2   Impact of technology, via counting the number of citations of the patent;
3   Linkages, via examining the counts of co-patenting patents;
4   University-industry-government linkages, via assessing the co-patenting patterns of these entities;
5   Science-based technology, via assessing the patents that cite scientific materials;
6   Comparative advantage, via examining the relative specialization index of a specific field of patenting; and
7   The knowledge base of technology, via examining the concordance of technology. This can be done by correlating emerging fields of patenting with other indicators (such as field of scientific research or industrial specialization).

This chapter capitalizes on patenting data to explore the knowledge landscape, as well as fusion of new technologies and industries that resulted from the convergence innovation process – as evident in the city innovation system. This chapter also provides analysis that relies on the historical series of the PCT (Patent Cooperation Treaty) patenting data extracted from the WIPO (World Intellectual Property Organization) database. It can illustrate the trend of patents applied by the entities of the region and thus provide reflection on the technological progress and pattern of convergence. The analysis will cover a considerable period of patenting trends, from January 1, 1997, to November 4, 2015. This allows exploration of the changes in the knowledge landscape in pursuit of technological knowledge.

    This study extends on that of Ng, Chandran, Wong and Shazana (2015) on exploration of knowledge clusters in selected regional innovation systems of Malaysia. It seeks to explore in-depth the evolution of knowledge landscapes of Kuala Lumpur and its important adjoining science and industrial park, Cyberjaya. In addition, this study highlights the entities (local firms, MNCs, universities or PRIs) which perform patenting activities in the city innovation system. We use Patsnap's knowledge landscaping tool to identify the keyword clustering and illustrate the knowledge landscape of the Kuala Lumpur innovation systems. The Patsnap tool is instrumental to this study, as it identifies keywords that appear in extracted patent documents and illustrates the intensity of specific clusters. A cluster is formed from grouping the most common keywords and is placed near other clusters that share similar keywords in a computer-generated, graphical landscape map. It also illustrates which entities perform in a specific cluster. In this study, we provide two timelines of knowledge landscapes – namely 1997 2005 and 1997 2015 to allow observation of changes within these two different periods.

As this chapter seeks to explore the knowledge ties that led to convergence innovation, we perform cross correlation analysis on the extracted patenting produced from the region. With each PCT patent assigned one or more IPC codes out of the thirty-five technological areas, we map the ties of patents produced from the region in order to highlight the fusion of technologies there. We then identify the knowledge ties and triangulate them with the innovation studies on Kuala Lumpur and Malaysia in the literature. These studies include the review of Malaysia's innovation system (Thiruchelvam, Chandran Ng and Wong, 2013 and Wong and Salmin, 2015); reported cases on city innovations of Kuala Lumpur (Mohamed, Fung and Wong, 2015 and Thiruchelvam et al., 2014); and development processes and policies of the city of Kuala Lumpur (Ramasamy et al., 2004 and Rimmer and Dick, 2009). The literature not only provides us with the background of innovation performance of various entities in Kuala Lumpur; it can also be useful as an account of the convergence patterns observed in the landscape map and knowledge ties.

For the case study, we provide the background and extract the main essence of our previous study on railway technology (Mohamed et al., 2015). As rail transport among urbanites in Kuala Lumpur is becoming more common, urban transit networks are being expanded. New transit lines are evidently being constructed from time to time. A case on what shapes the structure of a rail system is thus helpful to provide context on how convergence innovation takes place in the city innovation system of a developing country. The reported process in Mohamed et al. (2015) was analyzed through discussion with experts in a rail industrial firm, ERL of Malaysia. Several semi-structured interviews focusing on technological learning in order to achieve convergence innovation and process innovation were conducted. The experts include those who acquired tacit knowledge in electrification, rolling stock and signaling as well as those involved in the management process of R&D. The success factors maintained by the experts for convergence innovation in rail technology will be discussed in this chapter.

Our analytical chapter will first provide a background of innovation and production structures of the city of Kuala Lumpur and its adjoining science park, Cyberjaya. We then provide an overview of the patenting activities performed by entities located in Kuala Lumpur and Cyberjaya. This is followed by discussion on knowledge ties and fusion. Then, we present and describe the evolution of the knowledge landscape of Kuala Lumpur and Cyberjaya. The following section concludes.

3. Economic and technology structure of Kuala Lumpur and Cyberjaya

3.1 Economic structure

Kuala Lumpur is the national capital of Malaysia, located at the mid-west coast of Peninsular Malaysia. It is an enclave within the state of Selangor and is defined within the administrative borders of the federal government. It has been acknowledged as one of the most developed cities in terms of economy and income per capita. The Greater Kuala Lumpur project has recently been announced in the Economic Transformation Programme (ETP) to spur economic growth by creating a spillover avenue, via spreading out the economic activities of Kuala Lumpur to the adjoining cities and towns in the state of Selangor. The project seeks to create an urban agglomeration with a defined area covering ten municipalities. It also seeks to build infrastructure and supporting industries to ensure the spillover effect takes place at adjoining cities and towns, focusing on high-value-added services and high-tech industries. One of the approaches to create the spillover effect is to expand the high-speed rail and mass transit networks to reach more adjoining clusters around Kuala Lumpur, while constructing new transit lines to connect Kuala Lumpur with wider regional innovation systems around it.

Kuala Lumpur covers an area of 243km^2 with a total population of 1.73 million, of which its workforce numbers 887,200. The goal of developing Greater Kuala Lumpur is to expand the market for skilled professionals, via bridging the businesses of the working population in Kuala Lumpur with the defined agglomeration of the 7.9 million population. This will increase the segment of affluent consumers who are able to create value for firms, both in Kuala Lumpur and in its adjoining regions.

Kuala Lumpur had an economy of MYR 152,439 million (GDP) in 2013 (Department of Statistics, 2015). It has relatively more affluent consumers, with a GDP per capita of MYR 91,097 in 2013. Retail businesses owned by conglomerate firms – targeting the affluent consumer market – are commonly found in the city. The service sector dominates a large share of the GDP of Kuala Lumpur, contributing about 89 percent of the economy. Meanwhile, manufacturing is 5 percent, and other sectors such as agriculture, construction and mining are 5.6 percent of the economy. Kuala Lumpur attracted various MNCs such as IBM, Alstom, Vale and Schlumberger to set up regional headquarters there. Additionally, many financial businesses such as Citibank and HSBC have located their control function centers in Kuala Lumpur. Banking businesses are also common, with large banks such as Maybank, CIMB, RHB, Hong Leong and Public Bank having set up their headquarters in the city – in order to stay within close proximity to the central bank (Bank Negara) and the commodities exchange market in Kuala Lumpur.

Kuala Lumpur is also a region that appeals to multinationals running oil and gas industrial operations and commodities exchanges. Petronas and Shell – two major oil and gas players which have vertically integrated into both upstream (e.g. deepwater drilling and extraction) and downstream (e.g. refining, trading and marketing) operations – emerged as the key firms acting as anchors to the oil and gas agglomeration. Many activities of suppliers, producer servicing companies, engineering consultants and other entities performing supporting roles (such as universities and councils for oil and gas service) expanded within the anchor firms. Both local (e.g. Sapura Kencana and Scomi) and foreign (e.g. Technip, EP Engineering and Murphy) engineering consulting companies compete within close proximity of the anchor firms. There are also individuals who formerly worked at the anchor firms or consulting companies who have started producer servicing companies. They operate within and around the region to enjoy the economic spillover effect and to compete for subcontract projects. This phenomenon seems to correspond to Markusen's (1996) view on the hub-and-spoke industrial district.

Besides clusters of oil and gas industry related activities, Kuala Lumpur is also a platform for the operation and exchange of other commodities (e.g. rubber and palm oil). Two government agencies – namely, the Malaysian Palm Oil Board (MPOB) and Malaysian Rubber Board (MRB) – have set up their headquarters in Kuala Lumpur in order to promote and internationalize the plantation industries of Malaysia and perform research activities. These headquarters are hubs for technology transfer to firms around Malaysia. There are many plantation and biotechnology companies operating within the region. These include Oleon, Genting Plantations, TSH and Golden Hope. Many startup and spinoff companies originating from these firms and the plantation boards acquired niche business positions (Wong and Cheong, 2014, p. 389) and operate around the region, providing support and services to both local- and foreign-owned plantation industries.

While Singapore gained a relative advantage as a financial city by having many multinationals set up their regional headquarters for banking and financial services and operations there (Rimmer and Dick, 2009, p. 81), Kuala Lumpur's strength is as a hub for engineering services for oil and gas, plantations and commodities exchange. The environment attracts talent pools to perform various tasks including design and engineering tasks for upstream and downstream production; environmental engineering tasks; engineering tasks for transportation; professional services such as healthcare and legal matters; marketing and commercialization for various products and services; and research and development. Such diversity of business activities and interactions among the individuals and firms would likely lead to convergence innovations in different sectors.

3.2   *Science and technology base*

Malaysia initiated the special economic zone known as the Multimedia Super Corridor (MSC) in 1995. Here, techno-entrepreneurship would be spurred by supplying information-related technology and services with programs to build a cyber-savvy society. This would in turn create market demand for ICT (Ramasamy et al., 2004 and Rimmer and Dick, 2009, pp. 72–75). The MSC zone covers:

1 The Petronas Twin Towers in central Kuala Lumpur;
2 The Klang Valley which covers areas of Greater Kuala Lumpur and Putrajaya (the federal administrative cluster);
3 Technology Park Malaysia, a science park located in Kuala Lumpur to provide entrepreneurs and investors with a conducive environment – including engineering and ICT infrastructures and also research support from MIMOS (a research institute located in the centre of the park); and
4 Cyberjaya, a district modeled after Silicon Valley.

The MSC sought to create an ecosystem that would attract ICT investors and connect the supply from local companies to demand abroad. This led Kuala Lumpur to secure an average of 13 percent of the total annual national R&D budget. Kuala Lumpur together with Selangor secured an average of 48 percent over a ten-year period of time (Thiruchelvam et al. 2013, p. 20).

Technology Park Malaysia (TPM) was initiated to provide entrepreneurs investing in information and communication technology with advanced infrastructure and expert support services. It also welcomes those who invest in biotechnology and energy. MIMOS, a research institute endowed with substantial resources to perform R&D and patenting activities, has acquired a huge PCT patent portfolio related to ICT product development. TPM provides incubation services for new startups and offers various commercialization services via its entities, including the following:

1 TPM Biotech – product development, contract manufacturing, laboratory services related to biopharmaceutical products;
2 TPM Engineering – engineering design and solution, contract manufacturing, prototyping and rental for CNC machines; and
3 TPM IT – provision of broadband services, data centre, project management and consultancy related to ICT.

There are also many home-grown, high-tech companies that have located their headquarters and R&D unit at TPM, including the following:

4 IRIS – a company recognized for supporting the electronic passport and smart identity card project, and which has recently ventured into innovative farming and gas-powered waste disposal systems;
5 Other ICT startups investing in call services, cloud computing, content and animation, security, software, e-commerce and others;
6 Telco providers and media production and broadcasting companies;
7 Green technology startups such as Algaetech, a company focusing on the use of algae as a source of renewable energy; and
8 Healthcare and pharmaceutical startups.

Cyberjaya is another noteworthy science and industry park, launched in 1997 as the first hub of ICT activities in Malaysia. Covering an area of 28.94 km² and wired with state-of-the-art fiber optic technology, it is mandated to be the nucleus of the MSC. The Multimedia Development Corporation (MDeC) was incorporated in 1996 to govern the development of the MSC program and multimedia- and entrepreneurial-related activities in Cyberjaya. It is endowed with resources to oversee the growth prospects of Malaysia's digital economy and related development in Cyberjaya. Additionally, there are two universities located in Cyberjaya focusing on R&D for information and communication science and technology, as well as multimedia oriented training and education. While TPM attracts local startups searching for niches and developing indigenous technologies, Cyberjaya seems to be an attractive location for global control functions of MNCs. Many MNCs such as HSBC, DHL, Shell, Motorola, OCBC, IBM, Ericsson, BMW and Fujitsu located their business service and regional ICT operation units in Cyberjaya (Cyberjaya-tv, 2008 and World Finance, 2014). Cyberjaya has a population of seventy-five thousand out of which forty thousand are recognized as knowledge workers. The MSC companies in Cyberjaya generated a total revenue of MYR 7.22 billion in 2013, and thus has a revenue per capita of MYR 96,000 (CyberjayaMalaysia, 2015).

University of Malaya, a public research university located in Kuala Lumpur, is endowed with resources to provide tertiary education and basic research activities. The role of the university has been re-orientated – from educating, researching and performing knowledge transfer, to being recognized as an academic enterprise that seeks to instill graduates and faculty with a culture of creativity and innovation. It has an innovation center to provide graduates and faculty with the incubation facilities for commercialization of their research findings. University of Malaya has also been active in performing research and publication, witnessing an increase of patenting activities since 2009 as more graduates and faculty were granted institutional supports and funding for research commercialization (Wong and Salmin, 2015). The university has sought to build bridges connecting its research with industrial activities (particularly research related to healthcare, construction and engineering design, ICT, corporate strategic management and biotechnology) within the region.

3.3   *Patenting activities and convergence innovation*

Figure 8.1 plots the patenting trends by assignees affiliated with Kuala Lumpur and Cyberjaya. One can observe that there was a surge in applied patents in the year 2006, and another surge with much higher counts in 2009. The first surge can be attributed to the interest of firms to secure intellectual property protection of their inventions through a patent system that began to comply with the TRIPS agreement since 2004. The second surge is attributed to the wave of local research entities appearing in response to a Bayh-Dole like act that was launched in 2009. Many research institutions were granted resources to perform research

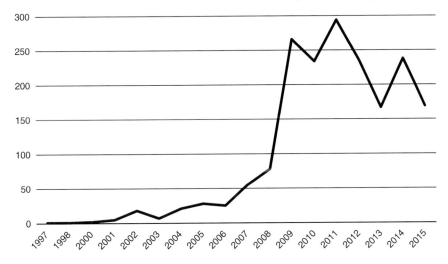

Figure 8.1 PCT patents by assignees from Kuala Lumpur and Cyberjaya (1997–2015)

and to commercialize research findings through licensing or startups based on patents. Researchers were encouraged to adopt a forward engineering approach, finding and building niches and creating markets via joint startup business entities with public universities and research institutes (Wong and Salmin, 2015). The technological push cycle is seen to have reached its ceiling in 2011, with the counts plummeting after that year. Even though the region has seen a dynamic production of patents over a period of eighteen years, Cyberjaya contributed only thirty patents over these two waves of patenting activities.

Computer technology, digital communication and measurement are found to be the most common technologies in Kuala Lumpur and Cyberjaya (Table 8.2). This can be partly attributed to patenting activities of MIMOS, which achieved astonishing results in PCT patent applications in these areas. MIMOS has outperformed many research institutes and productive firms in the region. Civil engineering, telecommunications and basic material chemistry follow as the next most common technologies. While telecommunication is correlated to the top three fields, civil engineering can be attributed to the clustered engineering and design businesses (such as oil and gas, infrastructure for transportation, etc.). Basic materials chemistry covers innovations related to liquid mixtures, such as petroleum or hydrocarbon gas mixtures and chemical substances used in plantations (such as herbicides, fertilizers, etc.). The innovations are related to the R&D activities performed to support the mining and hydrocarbon processing industries and various plantation businesses (such as oil palm, rubber, etc.). Semiconductor and electrical machinery are the technologies that complement the development of the top three dominant fields. Pharmaceutical and medical technology appear as the emerging technologies which support the growth of the healthcare industry.

Table 8.2 Fields of technology and patent counts for Kuala Lumpur and Cyberjaya (1997–2015)

Fields of Technology	Counts	Patents counts for MIMOS and its (%) of the total patents
Computer Technology	284	85 (30%)
Digital Communication	273	107 (39%)
Measurement	153	49 (32%)
Civil Engineering	102	1 (1%)
Telecommunications	91	29 (32%)
Basic Materials Chemistry	76	1 (1%)
Semiconductors	71	21 (30%)
Electrical Machinery	60	10 (17%)
Pharmaceuticals	57	–
Medical Technology	54	4 (7%)
Chemical Engineering	52	5 (10%)
Control	51	9 (18%)
Unclassified	42	4 (10%)
IT Methods for Management	41	8 (20%)
Other Special Machines	40	6 (15%)
Organic Fine Chemistry	39	14 (36%)
Macromolecular Chemistry, Polymers	36	3 (8%)
Biotechnology	33	–
Other Consumer Goods	28	–
Basic Communication Processes	26	12 (46%)
Mechanical Elements	26	–
Food Chemistry	25	–
Transport	23	–
Furniture, Games	22	–
Engines, Pumps, Turbines	20	1 (5%)
Optics	20	5 (25%)
Handling	19	–
Surface Technology, Coating	14	6 (43%)
Thermal Processes and Apparatus	14	2 (14%)
Microstructural, Nanotechnology	12	4 (33%)
Environmental Technology	11	–
Machine Tools	11	–
Materials, Metallurgy	9	–
Audio-visual Technology	8	4 (50%)
Textile and Paper Machines	2	–

Figure 8.2 illustrates the cross correlation map between the extracted patents based on IPC technology classification. The size of the bubble represents the density of patents in a particular field. The map allows us to analyze the fusion of different technologies that led to convergence innovation in Kuala Lumpur and

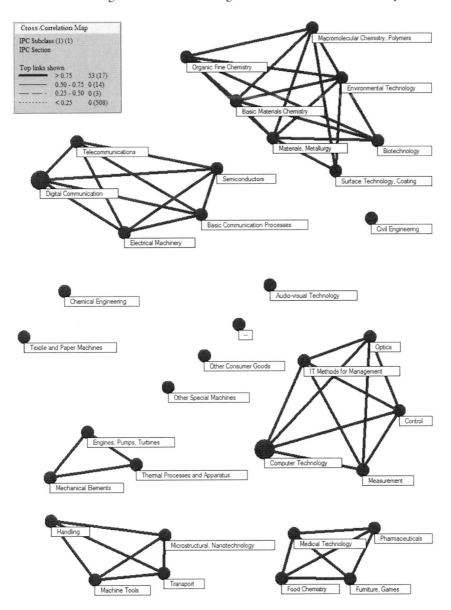

Figure 8.2 Cross correlation network map for fields of technology – Kuala Lumpur and Cyberjaya

Note: " –" denotes an unclassified field

Cyberjaya. There are basically six clusters that can be grouped into three major areas of industrial activity in Kuala Lumpur.

1   Computer and communication technologies: computer technology is dominant and co-exists with various techniques and methods in businesses (e.g. IT methods for technology, measurement and control) and applications of optical technologies (e.g. optics). Digital communication technology also appears to be dominant and co-exists with various communication technologies (e.g. telecommunication and basic communication processes) and semiconductor and electrical machinery (e.g. electrical and electrical machinery).
2   Pharmaceutical and process innovations: co-existence of various types of process- and system- and chemical-oriented innovations, including with material and chemical technologies (e.g. basic material chemistry, materials and metallurgy, surface technology and coating, biotechnology, environmental technology, macromolecular chemistry and polymers and organic fine chemistry).
3   Pharmaceuticals: co-exists and clustered with different kinds of technologies, including medical technology, food chemistry and furniture and games.
4   Machinery, tools and nanotechnology: relatively small clustered network that consists of thermal processes and apparatus, engines, pumps and turbines and mechanical elements.
5   Process innovation (handling): with machine tools, transport and research-oriented innovation such as microstructural and nanotechnology.

Figure 8.3 (a) and (b) exhibit the knowledge clusters that are mapped based on keywords found in extracted patent documents. Each figure represents a period of time, one for 1997–2005 and another one for 1997–2015. The patenting activities for 1997–2005 seem to have focused on a few fragmented technologies – one on rubber-related innovations ("latex, rubber, CU, materials, concentrate"), one on ICT for security purposes ("individual, biometrics, electronically, verify, identification", "network, biometric, message, cell, bed"), and others focusing on electrical mechanical elements (see Figure 8.3[a]). The patenting activities are dominated by local firms. The patent counts from government-related organization, PRIs and universities were insignificant.

Figure 8.3(b) illustrates the landscape of the following growth in patenting activities. Many clusters are seen connected with each other (clusters are marked and displayed side by side). This displays the different processes of convergence of innovation in this period of time. While many patent counts are attributed to PRIs, considerable patent applications were also made by local firms and MNCs for the following period. Three clusters – namely "sensor, electrode, oil, test, palm", "implant, dental, palm, extract, oil" and "energy, harvester, light, cell, generator" – emerged as the dominant clusters with a high density of applied patents. The convergence processes were led by PRIs and universities (implant, dental, palm, extract, oil). We observe that there are local firms participating in building these niches.

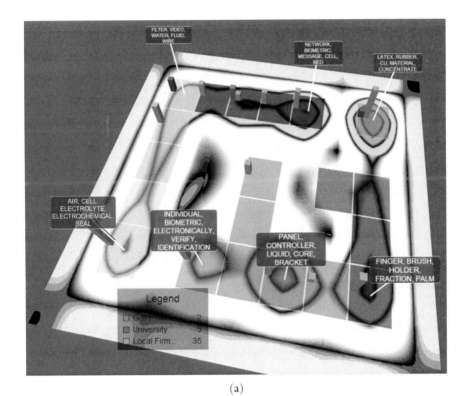

(a)

(b)

Figure 8.3 Knowledge cluster mapping of patenting activities of Kuala Lumpur and Cyberjaya: (a) 1997–2005; (b) 1997–2015

The footprints of PRIs appear in almost all clusters and are particularly evident in network-, communication- and visualization-related technologies. We observe the lead held by PRIs with some local firms in converging innovations between sensor technology and process innovation in oil palm ("sensor, electrode, oil, test, palm"). PRIs also seem to have dominated clean energy innovation ("energy, harvester, light, cell, generator"). The footprints of MNCs and local firms seem to be in technologies that respond to immediate market demand, such as rubber; oil palm and fat; hydrocarbon and various mechanical systems that are useful for transport; mining and refinery processes; and machinery and equipment ("rubber, oil, latex, water, palm", "fluid, mould, formation, filter, control" and "stream, hydrocarbon, cool, turbine, engine"). These clusters can be attributed to engineering, design and business activities in the industrial agglomeration of Kuala Lumpur. We observe footprints of PRIs and universities in these clusters, suggesting the interest of these entities in venturing into niches that correspond to the industry interest and market demand. This suggests a matching process between those (from PRIs and universities) who perform in response to technology push forces, and those who respond to market demand. The process involved cooperation of various entities (university, MNCs, local firms, etc.) for joint research and co-patenting activities.

4.   Case investigation into railway technology

This section seeks to understand how convergence innovation possibly could take place in a city. Unless otherwise noted, what follows is drawn from our previous study on rail technology (Mohamed et al., 2015). The case in point would be the recognition of the importance of an integrated rail system to stimulate growth and development in the urban area and alleviate traffic congestion. A Malaysian rail company, Express Rail Link Sdn Bhd (ERL), which was incorporated in 1997, had sought to obtain rail technology knowledge via importing high-speed rail technology from Siemens to link Kuala Lumpur International Airport with Kuala Lumpur city. It then attained operational and maintenance capability for a high-speed rail. We report the process of convergence that ultimately led to the export of services abroad.

The high-speed rail technology adopted by ERL was achieved via a concession agreement to finance, design, construct, operate and maintain the daily high-speed rail service. In 1999, ERL had set-up a subsidiary, E-MAS, to operate and maintain the high-speed railway system. The subsidiary was started as a joint-venture (JV) entity between Siemens (51 percent ownership) and ERL (49 percent).[1] E-MAS recruited an initial batch of seasoned engineers – such as those with backgrounds in aviation industries or familiar with military technology – who brought the technical knowledge on rail and rail-related engineering. The recruitment process was directed by Siemens's guidelines on what skills and knowledge are needed to operate a high-speed rail system.

The main components and the core technologies of rail are easily accessible in the Malaysian market. This is attributed to the supplier industries that used to participate in infrastructure building projects or had invested in transportation technology. Nonetheless, we observe that the process of knowledge accumulation is at the starting point (at the end of the 1990s), at which time the knowledge for operation and maintenance of the rail system was limited. Convergence is not evident at this early point. The R&D activities are rather limited, as most employees and engineers adhered to the Standard Operating Procedures (SOPs) outlined by Siemens.

Over a period of training and learning about rail technology in E-MAS, assimilation of knowledge about ERL railway systems took place and occurred in instances during the 2000s. These include the following:

- integration of the rolling stock component with track work technology to ensure that the high-speed trains move stably on the tracks;
- integration of in-train control and communications; and
- integration of electrification and information systems to provide high-safety features and on-time information to operators and passengers.

The convergence instances are attributed to the consistent efforts of E-MAS in upgrading their human capital workforce. E-MAS engineers and technical personnel are encouraged to interact regularly with those who have worked on other rail projects. Some who attained specific tacit knowledge of rail systems were absorbed and recruited into its workforce as part of its searching effort for new niches. The knowledge from the railway projects spilled over to E-MAS via human capital mobility. The knowledge gained via human capital development and recruitment of skilled workers helped E-MAS to propagate technical knowledge and create a productive structure, useful for rail operation and maintenance tasks.

Another impetus that propelled the knowledge accumulation is the high usage of trains, which affects the operation of the rail system. The mileage accumulated through train operation reached a critical point, whereby ERL's Siemens trains were the first in the world to reach the scheduled overhaul for maintenance. Since ERL trains reached the critical mileage earlier than counterparts elsewhere, the overhaul was the first of its series and was handled by the E-MAS engineers who worked closely with Siemens. The ability to carry out this sort of maintenance service suggests a high level of technical capability attained by E-MAS. E-MAS also searched for other maintenance procedures that might add value to the maintenance procedures handed down by Siemens. The engineers then incorporated these other forms of maintenance activities to preserve the operational condition of the system. One example we learned about is the scheduled monitoring task to ensure there are no electricity leaks at overhead catenary poles. E-MAS used a thermal photography technique to screen poles for suspected leaks.

The capability attained by E-MAS then led them to venture into new businesses. It now offers railway maintenance services to other countries in the form of technical, operational and maintenance consultation. An example of a technical maintenance service that is subscribed to abroad is the installation of overhead catenary poles in the Thai air rail link (which was constructed with the support of Siemens' technology). Another example is the Makkah-Madinah rail link, which procures the services of E-MAS to strengthen its operations during the pilgrimage period.

5.   Major findings and conclusions

We have reviewed the evolution of knowledge structures and highlighted the knowledge clusters that were derived from the research activities (performed by research entities such as public research institutes and universities) and the industrial and engineering activities. We underlined the importance of convergence innovation in acquiring the desired structure of a knowledge economy. Our analysis on knowledge landscapes of Kuala Lumpur and its adjoining science and industrial park, Cyberjaya, informed the literature on the types of knowledge ties in a city innovation system, and the fusion of knowledge that led to new niches and industries.

We provided a case study to inform readers about how convergence innovation might possibly take place in a city innovation system. Convergence innovation takes place in a city with a broad base of industries – the city witnesses a diversification of different activities from time to time and, thus, fuses together niches and expertise. Those who carry tacit knowledge or specialized skills are most likely to be recruited by knowledge-driven organizations to lead specific tasks and technology development. They interact with experts who specialize in specific technologies and assimilate technology from abroad, in order to develop a process that allows the emergence of convergence innovation. This is evident in the case of ERL's subsidiary that attained the ability to operate and maintain a high-speed rail system and subsequently venture its businesses abroad, providing consultation and high-value-added services to firms that aspire to operate and maintain their own rail systems.

While the case seems insufficient to allow a strong generalization on how convergence takes place, it suggests a pattern of searching efforts for knowledge and convergence of technology. Future research reporting on cases of convergence of innovation may provide more insight and understanding on how convergence of different technologies takes place. Such understanding can be useful for corporate managers, techno-entrepreneurs and engineers to appropriate the process of convergence, as well as for policymakers to provide an environment or structure that is conducive for convergence innovation.

Note

1 The contractual JV ended in June 2005. ERL has since then taken over Siemens's shares of the company.

References

Autio, E. (1998), "Evaluation of RTD in regional systems of innovation", *European Planning Studies*, vol. 6, no. 2, pp. 131–140.

Bernadas, A. T. and Albuquerque, E. M. (2003), "Cross-over, thresholds, and inter-actions between science and technology: Lessons for less-developed countries", *Research Policy*, vol. 32, no. 5, pp. 865–885.

Bresnahan, T., Gambardella, A. and Saxenian, A. L. (2005), "'Old economy' inputs for 'new economy' outcomes: Cluster formation in the new Silicon Valleys", in Breschi, F. and Malerba, F. (eds.), *Clusters, Networks and Innovation*, pp. 113–135, Oxford: Oxford Univ. Press.

Clare, K. (2013), "The essential role of place within the creative industries: Boundaries, networks and play", *Cities*, vol. 34, pp. 52–57.

Cooke, P., Uranga, M. G. and Etxebarria, G. (1997), "Regional innovation system: Institutional and organizational dimensions", *Research Policy*, vol. 26, no. 4/5, pp. 475–491.

CyberjayaMalaysia (2015), *Business Overview*, access on 29 Nov, 2015 at www.cyberjayamalaysia.com.my/business/overview

Cyberjaya-tv (2008), *Cyberjaya Malaysia's IT-Themed City*, access on 29 Nov, 2015 at www.cyberjaya-tv.com/2008/CYBERJAYA_MALAYSIA_IT_THEMED_CITY.html

Department of Statistics (2015), *GDP by States*, access on 29 Nov, 2015 at www.statistics.gov.my/index.php?r=column/cdatavisualization&menu_id=WjJMQ1F0N3RXclNGNWpIODBDRmh2UT09&bul_id=eHV2QXd0RC9rdi9uenJhL2hoaytNQT09

Fagerberg, J., Srholec, M. and Knell, M. (2007), "The competitiveness of nations: Why some countries prosper while others fall behind", *World Development*, vol. 35, no. 10, pp. 1595–1620.

Foray, D. (2006), *The Economics of Knowledge*, Cambridge: MIT Press.

Grupp, H. (1996), "Spillover effects and the science base of innovations reconsidered: An empirical approach", *Journal of Evolutionary Economics*, vol. 6, no. 2, pp. 175–197.

Grupp, H. (1998), *Foundations of the Economics of Innovation: Theory, Measurement and Practice*, Northampton: Edward Elgar.

Hacklin, F., Marxt, C. and Fahni, F. (2009), "Co-evolutionary cycles of convergence: An extrapolation from the ICT industry", *Technological Forecasting and Social Change*, vol. 76, no. 6, pp. 723–736.

Intarakumnerd, P. (2011), "Two models of research technology organizations in Asia", *Science, Technology and Society*, vol. 16, no. 1, pp. 11–28.

Islam, N. and Ozcan, S. (2015), "The management of nanotechnology: Analysis of technology linkages and the regional nanotechnology competencies", *R&D Management*, http://onlinelibrary.wiley.com/doi/10.1111/radm.12161/abstract.

Jaffe, A. and Trajtenberg, M. (2002), *Patents, Citations and Innovation: A Window on the Knowledge Economy*, Cambridge: MIT Press.

Karvonen, M. and Kassi, T. (2013), "Patent citations as a tool for analyzing the early stages of convergence", *Technological Forecasting and Social Change*, vol. 80, no. 6, pp. 1094–1107.

Kim, L. (1997), *Imitation to Innovation, the Dynamics of Korea's Technological Learning*, Boston: Harvard Business School Press.

Lee, K. (2013), *Schumpeterian Analysis of Economic Catch-Up: Knowledge, Path-Creation, and the Middle-Income Trap*, Cambridge: Cambridge University Press.

Lee, K.-R. (2015), "Toward a new paradigm of technological innovation: Convergence innovation", *Asian Journal of Technology Innovation*, vol. 23, no. 1, pp. 1–8.

Malerba, F. and Mani, S. (2009) (eds.), *Sectoral Systems of Innovation and Production in Developing Countries: Actors, Structure and Evolution*, Cheltenham: Edward Elgar.

Markatou, M. and Alexandrou, E. (2015), "Urban system of innovation: Main agents and main factors of success", *Procedia – Social and Behavioral Sciences*, vol. 195, pp. 240–250.

Markusen, A. (1996), "Sticky places in slippery space: A typology of industrial districts", *Economic Geography*, vol. 72, no. 3, pp. 293–313.

Mathews, J. and Cho, D.-S. (2000), *Tiger Technology: The Creation of a Semiconductor Industry in East Asia*, Cambridge: Cambridge University Press.

Mohamed, M., Tung, H.-N. and Wong, C. Y. (2015), "Convergence innovation in railway technology: How ERL of Malaysia attained its co-evolution structure for systemic development", *Asian Journal of Technology Innovation*, vol. 23, no. 1, pp. 93–108.

Nesta, L. and Patel, P. (2004), "National patterns of technological accumulation: Use of patent statistics", in Moed, H. F., Glanzel, W. and Schmoch, U. (eds.), *Handbook of Quantitative Science and Technology Research: The Use of Publication and Patent statistics in Studies of S&T Systems*, pp. 531–552, Dordrecht: Kluwer Academic Publisher.

Ng, B.-K., Chandran, V.G.R., Wong, C.-Y. and Shazana, A. (2015), *Cluster Innovation and Development in Malaysia: Learning, Network and Institution*, Kuala Lumpur: Draft prepared for submission for Consideration for Book Publication by UM Press.

Odagiri, H., Goto, A., Sunami, A. and Nelson, N. N. (2010) (eds.), *Intellectual Property Rights, Development and Catch-Up: An International Comparative Study*, Oxford: Oxford University Press.

Porter, M. (1998), "Clusters and the new economics of competition", *Harvard Business Review*, vol. 76, no. 6, pp. 77–90.

Potter, K., Whittington, K. B. and Powell, W. W. (2005), "The institutional embeddedness of high-tech regions: Relational foundations of the Boston biotechnology community", in Breschi, F. and Malerba, F. (eds.), *Clusters, Networks and Innovation*, pp. 261–296, Oxford: Oxford University Press.

Ramasamy, B., Chakrabarty, A. and Cheah, M. (2004), "Malaysia's leap into the future: An evaluation of the multimedia super corridor", *Technovation*, vol. 24, pp. 871–883.

Rimmer, P. J. and Dick, H. (2009), *The City in Southeast Asia: Patterns, Processes and Policy*, Singapore: NUS Press.

Schmoch, U. (2007), "Double-boom cycles and the comeback of science-push and market-pull", *Research Policy*, vol. 36, no. 7, pp. 1000–1015.

Sorenson, O. (2005), "Social networks and the persistence of clusters: Evidence from the computer workstation industry", in Breschi, F. and Malerba, F. (eds.), *Clusters, Networks and Innovation*, pp. 297–316, Oxford: Oxford Univ. Press.

Steinmueller, E. (2014), "Expanding the innovation frontier: Cultivating diversity and creativity", presented at *11th Asialics Conference* on 25 Sept, 2014, Daegu.

Su, Y.-S. and Wu, F.-S., (2015), "Regional systems of biotechnology innovation – the case of Taiwan", *Technological Forecasting and Social Change*, vol. 100, pp. 96–106.

Tang, W.-S. (2015), "Creative industries, public engagement and urban redevelopment in Hong Kong: Cultural regeneration as another dose of Isotopia?", *Cities*, http://www.sciencedirect.com/science/article/pii/S0264275115001390.

Teubal, M. and Andersen, E. (2000), "Enterprise restructuring and embeddedness: A policy and systems perspective", *Industrial and Corporate Change*, vol. 9, no. 1, pp. 87–111.

Thiruchelvam, K., Chandran, V.G.R., Ng, B.-K. and Wong, C.-Y. (2013), *Malaysia's Quest for Innovation: Progress and Lessons Learned*, Petaling Jaya: SIRD.

Thiruchelvam, K., Hassan, N., Daud, M. N., Mohd, I., Inangda, N., Yusoff, S. M., Aziz, A. A., Ahmand, F., Hanif, N. R. and Wong, C.-Y. (2014), *City Innovation Systems: Case Studies on Urban Innovations in Kuala Lumpur, Malaysia*, Petaling Jaya: Gerakbudaya Enterprise.

Vona, F. and Consoli, D. (2014), "Innovation and skill dynamics: A life-cycle approach", *Industrial and Corporate Change*, vol. 24, no. 6, pp. 1393–1415.

Wang, N. and Hagedoorn, J. (2014), "The lag structure of the relationship between patenting and internal R&D revisited", *Research Policy*, vol. 43, no. 8, pp. 1275–1285.

Wong, C.-Y., Chandran, V.G.R. and Ng, B.-K. (2014), "Technology diffusion in the telecommunications services industry of Malaysia", *Information Technology for Development*, http://www.tandfonline.com/doi/abs/10.1080/02681102.2014.949611?journalCode=titd20.

Wong, C.-Y. and Cheong, K.-C. (2014), "Diffusion of catching-up industrialization strategies: The dynamics of East Asia's policy learning process", *Journal of Comparative Asian Development*, vol. 13, no. 3, pp. 369–404.

Wong, C.-Y. and Goh, K.-L. (2012), "The evolution and pathways for development: Science and technology of NIEs and selected Asian emerging countries", *Scientometrics*, vol. 92, no. 3, pp. 523–548.

Wong, C.-Y., Hu, M.-C. and Shiu, J.-W. (2015), "Collaboration between public research institutes and universities: A study of industrial technology research institute, Taiwan", *Science, Technology and Society*, vol. 20, no. 2, pp. 161–181.

Wong, C.-Y. and Salmin, M. (2015), "Attaining a productive structure for technology: The Bayh–Dole effect on university–industry–government relations in developing economy", *Science and Public Policy*, vol. 43, pp. 29–45.

Wong, P.-K. (2011) (ed.), *Academic Entrepreneurship in Asia: The Role and Impact Universities in National Innovation Systems*, Cheltenham: Edward Elgar.

World Finance (2014), *Intelligent City Cyberjaya Rises to Become the 'Silicon Valley of Malaysia'*, access on 29 Nov, 2015 at www.worldfinance.com/wealth-management/real-estate/living-in-cyberjaya-the-silicon-valley-of-malaysia

Yusuf, S. and Nabeshima, K. (2005), "Creative industries in East Asia", *Cities*, vol. 22, no. 2, pp. 109–122.

9 Summary and policy implications

Kong-rae Lee

1. Summary and concluding remarks

Few studies have investigated convergence innovation, which has little discovered and proposed new theories or hypotheses. This situation motivated the authors to further explore the issue in this book and understand the process of convergence in order to efficiently manage and utilize its outcome for human beings or organizations. Throughout this book, it is pointed out that important elements of the convergence process are learning, networks and communications, and to manage them well is crucial in creating convergence innovation. Convergence processes need to be strategically managed not only at the firm level but also at the meso and the country levels.

This book deals with many issues through individual, organizational, meso and country level analyses. It also investigates a group of agendas such as how individuals and firms learn and diffuse knowledge as origins of convergence innovation; how to navigate the processes of convergence innovation; and case investigations into Asian industries and countries. The results of the investigations and their arguments are summarized as follows.

First, the processes of convergence begin from individuals so that exploring the processes at the personal level is necessary. It starts when a researcher with a cognitive map interacts with another researcher holding a different cognitive map. Individuals behave by modes of learning and evolve one after another. Technological learning has gone beyond the simple mode of learning-by-doing, to learning-by-porting via learning-by-using and learning-by-integration, producing convergence innovation.

Second, collective learning is the most important for successful convergence processes. The interaction among individuals evolves into a collective learning that creates new knowledge. Under active learning, the applications of a given technology are so diverse that the convergence to create new functions, products and services becomes possible. Managing convergence innovation is mainly concerned with this collective learning at the firm level. Especially, large firms have many hardships that became obstacles in pursuing convergence innovation. To create convergence innovation, they have to cope with the anxiety caused by changes and convergences, the objectives and visions for changes, and the images that follow changes.

Third, different types of convergence innovation emerge depending upon firm-specific learning modes and growth strategies. Inside-out type of convergence innovation arises when firms try to utilize their core competence for exploiting business opportunities in other areas, while the outside-in type prevails when firms are in a booming period as they diligently integrate outside technologies in order to solve their own technological problems.

Fourth, networks and communications matter for convergence since they are means to diffuse convergence throughout the organizations and societies. Individuals come up with new innovations through various networks with cognitive processes and communications. Knowledge, information and innovations spread within and between organizations through digital media, such as e-mail, and are adopted in much the same way as they are from an external source. Networks and communications facilitate and accommodate individual needs, tastes or personal situations, but they also allow dis-adoption due to the dissatisfaction with the innovation or substitution by a newer innovation that better meets the individual's needs or desires, leading to more convergence.

Fifth, diversity is an important enabling factor in navigating convergence innovation. Diversity makes major steps in managing convergence innovation and often involves creating a space of freedom and opportunity. It is proposed in the context of Asian countries, a transformational change for growing out of the heritage of catching-up and competitiveness agenda and seeking for diversification to be an important agenda for promoting convergence innovation. In this aspect, a strategy of greater diversification remains an option for Korea as a response to the risk associated with the current dominance of the catching-up industries and the uneven inter-sectoral performance.

Sixth, a geographical factor with clustering of firms and professionals is an important element for convergence innovation. A city innovation system matters because it creates a path for convergence. As in the cases of Kuala Lumpur and Cyberjaya of Malaysia, a railway company initially assimilated rail technology to attain capability in operation and maintenance. As time went by, a group of firms in the railroad industry clustered and learned together, upgrading their level of technology. As a result, convergence innovation of the company was evident throughout the period of the 2000s. The knowledge ties among firms clustering in a large city enabled the emergence of convergence innovation.

Last, we found that intra-industry convergence has been prevailing in contemporary industrial innovation. However, inter-industry convergence has been rapidly arising between different industry types. The specialized suppliers sector showed the highest degree of intra-convergence innovation, implying that it has been the focal point of convergence innovation, integrating forward and backward industries. From the cross-country comparison (China, Japan, Korea and Taiwan), no major differences in the characteristics of convergence innovation between countries were discovered, implying that inherent industrial and technological characteristics may play a critical role in convergence activities regardless of country specific features.

2.   Policy implications

The summary and concluding remarks above imply that taking diverse viewpoints is necessary in order to promote convergence innovation. Policies are generally directed to promoting specific industries or technologies for economic growth or to improving people's welfare. Policies here indicate innovation policies for encouraging convergence innovation. Policy implications here have been drawn from seven perspectives: spatial, process, user-supplier, R&D, human side, institutional and cultural. We hope that these seven perspectives provide better insights for local and central governments in pursuing convergence innovation.

On the spatial perspective

Research findings that a city innovation system matters in encouraging convergence provide a policy implication that such knowledge-creating agents as research institutes, corporate R&D centers, universities and so forth should be geographically clustered as much as possible in city regions. Past innovation studies with a cluster approach did not clearly show what scope of geographical area needs to be taken into account in locating knowledge-creating organizations. It is believed that a well-functioning city innovation system effectively creates a path for convergence innovation. The arguments made in Chapter 8 imply that a large city can be a location in scope in clustering them for successful convergence innovation. This point also needs to be considered when firms globalize their R&D – for instance, sourcing diverse knowledge by locating R&D centers in talented regions.

On the process perspective

As argued repeatedly in this book, learning, particularly collective learning, is important in managing the processes of convergence at the organizational level. Firms that pursue convergence innovations require policy tools to make institutions well adapted for effective learning. For example, training and rewarding talented project leaders capable of managing R&D projects and teams are likely to be critical. They are to be well equipped with knowledge and leadership to manage the processes of convergence in order to deal with conflicts or problems arising from the gap in knowledge among research personnel or from the different stages of the process. In addition to training and rewarding of the talented project leaders, firms need to have policy tools to do the gate-keeping function as well. For instance, building up and maintaining linkages between in-side and out-side professionals through forums and regular seminars is a way of facilitating collective learning and managing convergence processes.

At the country level, governments should encourage cooperation among individuals, firms, research institutes and universities. Taking a process perspective means carefully managing each stage of convergence processes. Careful consideration of people and organizations during the convergence processes leads to more frequent cooperation and exchange of knowledge among them, as do their convergences. Governments have so far emphasized competition rather than cooperation among R&D personnel and organizations, which has obviously increased R&D productivity, but they have failed to encourage cooperation so as to generate meaningful innovation. Designing such policies for encouraging cooperation requires more policy research, resources and creative ideas, which need extra space, time, allowance, margin and so forth.

On the user-supplier perspective

The user-supplier perspective is to incorporate diverse users' and suppliers' knowledge into the process of convergence innovation. It emphasizes the downstream side of the innovation process like early integration of users and suppliers' role at the organizational level. The importance of user-supplier interaction has been much emphasized in innovation studies as a source of successful innovation. It is likely to become even more important in convergence innovation. Policies of companies and governments intended to foster convergence should seriously take ideas and viewpoints of users into consideration, in addition to those of suppliers. Government-led projects are usually ignorant of user-side ideas so that their results are neither innovative nor sufficient to fulfil originally designed purposes. Therefore, the role of lead users and user-supplier interaction should be considered from the very beginning of a policy-designing process and implemented for the purpose of achieving policy targets.

On the R&D perspective

R&D is a good instrument for targeting specific convergence innovation. Planning R&D projects with convergence nature or targets is an effective way of making convergence innovation, assuming that it will be followed by actual implementation. Scientists and engineers generally tend to focus on issues of their own discipline in doing R&D. Thus, the portion of R&D projects with convergence nature is likely to be low if they are allowed to perform them autonomously. One way to promote convergence R&D is to intentionally plan R&D with convergence nature. Nowadays a substantial portion of government R&D projects and programs have characteristics of convergence. This is because they have not only interdisciplinary nature, but also their objectives require convergence of diverse knowledge. Social and technological problems to be solved by governments in reality are so complicated and complex that they need convergence of diverse knowledge, and so do R&D projects. Government officials in charge of R&D planning therefore need to obtain in-depth knowledge on convergence innovation.

On the human side perspective

The human side factors determining successful convergence are many, including manpower training, general education of people, leaders and their leadership, networks, communications, cooperation and conflict resolution among people, and credibility, creativity, and braveness of people to achieve something complex and complicated. Especially university education at the graduate school level needs to be emphasized for making policies to encourage convergence innovation. Through proper education, future professionals may be well harmonized with each other in respect to diversity in mind and with readiness to do convergence projects. Above-mentioned qualities of people conducive to convergence should be cultivated in the education system over a long period of time. Communications and cooperation among people, both at intra and inter organizational levels, are critically important for convergence, so they need to be culturally encouraged and strengthened. They are also likely to be amicably accelerated by capable leaders and encouraging organizational culture.

On the institutional perspective

This perspective concerns institutions associated with promotion, compensation, protection, co-exploitation of convergence innovation and so on. A set of institutions that enables people to create or configure convergence that fits into the unique culture of the country or the organization should be identified, formulated and built up by policies. At the company level, creation of convergence innovation depends much upon how many experienced and talented project leaders capable of managing diverse projects are available. Therefore, firms need to have competitive institutions to select and train such capable project leaders. Not only leaders but also members of organizations and societies require credibility, creativity and bravery to achieve a higher level of convergence innovation. In this regard, whether a national innovation system equipped with institutions to nurture human-side characteristics of such leaders and people exists or not is important for fostering convergence innovation. Governments should obviously orient their policies towards this direction by designing and building up various institutions conducive to convergence innovation.

On the cultural perspective

This perspective concerns a mindset such as creation of community values and social norms, and the trust relationship of stake holders, decision making of collective agents, and so on. Whether or not organizations or science and technology communities have a culture to adapt to diversity is critical in making convergence innovation. An autonomous environment is definitely required in R&D communities for convergence because it helps generate creative ideas. Likewise, democratic leadership, democratic culture and democratic decision making rather than dictatorial ones are likely to create more convergence. In this respect, people should enjoy freedom as much as possible both in organizations and in communities unless they exert negative influence. A liberal working environment should also be respected, and regulations should be minimized. At the country level, a democratic political system may have a higher possibility to develop such culture than any other regimes.

We hope that our findings will provide a clue to developing innovation policies and expanding theories on various aspects of convergence innovation. Innovation studies that focused on convergence need to deepen the research framework incorporating various perspectives in the future. Research findings of this book might provide useful insights into the exploration and exploitation of future convergence studies. However, this book certainly has some limitations because we did not have enough evidence on sources, processes and outcomes of convergence innovation at the firm, industry and country levels. To make sure that arguments and analytical results of this book are right and correct, similar analyses can be extended to additional countries in more recent times and additional cases of firms and industries in convergence innovation can be included.

Index